Living by the Book

Also by James Montgomery Boice

Witness and Revelation in the Gospel of John
Philippians: An Expositional Commentary
The Sermon on the Mount
How to Live the Christian Life (originally, *How to Live It Up*)
Ordinary Men Called by God (originally, *How God Can Use Nobodies*)
The Last and Future World
The Gospel of John: An Expositional Commentary (5 volumes in one)
"Galatians" in the *Expositor's Bible Commentary*
Can You Run Away from God?
Our Sovereign God, editor
Our Savior God: Studies on Man, Christ and the Atonement, editor
Does Inerrancy Matter?
The Foundation of Biblical Authority, editor
Making God's Word Plain, editor
The Epistles of John
Genesis: An Expositional Commentary (3 volumes)
The Parables of Jesus
The Christ of Christmas
The Minor Prophets: An Expositional Commentary (2 volumes)
Standing on the Rock
The Christ of the Open Tomb
Foundations of the Christian Faith (4 volumes in one)
Christ's Call to Discipleship
Transforming Our World: A Call to Action, editor
Ephesians: An Expositional Commentary
Daniel: An Expositional Commentary
Joshua: We Will Serve the Lord
Nehemiah: Learning to Lead
The King Has Come
Romans (4 volumes)
Mind Renewal in a Mindless Age
Amazing Grace
Psalms (2 of 3 volumes)
Sure I Believe, So What!
Hearing God When You Hurt
Two Cities / Two Loves
Here We Stand: A Call from Confessing Evangelicals, editor,
    with Benjamin E. Sasse

Living by the Book

*The Joy of Loving
and Trusting God's Word*

Based on Psalm 119

James Montgomery Boice

Baker Books

A Division of Baker Book House Co
Grand Rapids, Michigan 49516

© 1997 by James Montgomery Boice

Published by Baker Books
a division of Baker Book House Company
P.O. Box 6287, Grand Rapids, MI 49516-6287

Third printing, December 2000

Printed in the United States of America

Library of Congress Cataloging-in-Publication Data

Boice, James Montgomery, 1938-
    Living by the book : the joy of loving and trusting God's
word ; based on Psalm 119 / James Montgomery Boice.
        p.   cm.
    Includes bibliographical references.
    ISBN 0-8010-5758-2 (paper)
    1. Bible. O.T. Psalms CXIX—Criticism, interpretation, etc.
    2. Christian life. I. Title.
    BS1450 119th.B65   1977
    223'.206—dc21   96-47820

For current information about all releases from Baker Book House, visit our web
site:

                        http://www.bakerbooks.com

To HIM
who is the faithful and true witness
the ruler of God's creation

Contents

Preface   9

Psalm 119
1. First Things First (verses 1–8)   11
2. Starting Young (verses 9–16)   21
3. Trials on the Way (verses 17–32)   31
4. In God's School (verses 33–40)   43
5. Finding God in His Word (verses 41–64)   55
6. Affliction (verses 65–88)   67
7. The Eternal Word (verses 89–96)   79
8. Loving God's Word (verses 97–104)   89
9. The Clarity of God's Word (verses 105–12)   101
10. Walking by God's Word (verses 113–28)   113
11. God's Wonderful Words (verses 129–44)   125
12. Using God's Word in Prayer (verses 145–52)   137
13. Obedience while Waiting (verses 153–68)   149
14. This Poor Sheep (verses 169–76)   161

Notes   173

Preface

ABOUT TWO-THIRDS OF THE WAY THROUGH THE BOOK OF Psalms the student of Scripture comes on both the shortest psalm in the Psalter, which is also the shortest chapter in the Bible, and two psalms later the longest psalm, which is also the longest chapter. The first is Psalm 117. It has two verses and five lines. The second is Psalm 119. It has 176 verses and 315 lines. Psalm 117 tells us to praise God. Psalm 119 praises God for the gift of his Word, which is one of the chief reasons we should praise him. This is because it is only through the Bible that we can come to know who God is and learn to live an upright Christian life.

Over the years many great Bible teachers have been drawn to this psalm. John Calvin, the chief theologian of the Reformation period, preached twenty-two sermons on Psalm 119, one for each of the psalm's twenty-two sections. He preached them in Geneva, Switzerland, between January 8 and June 2, 1553. Charles Bridges, a British evangelical of the last century, matched Calvin with a large study, also twenty-two chapters. Thomas Manton won the prize. He was one of the Puritans and was quite prolific, as were many of them. He wrote three massive volumes on this psalm, running to more than 1,600 pages with 190 sermons—more than one sermon per verse.

In my judgment, scholarly and pastoral acclaim of this nature is completely justified, for Psalm 119 is truly a great psalm, a masterpiece of devout reflection on the nature, blessing, and glory of the Word of God.

We live in a day when people do not much value God's Word, even in evangelical churches. We say that we value it, but our neglect of the Word belies our confession. We do not spend much time in serious Bible study. We do not memorize God's Word, hiding it in our hearts, as the psalmist says he did. As for today's preachers, many of them also neglect the Word, thinking that it will not appeal to mass audiences and that serious Bible teaching will harm their churches' growth. They turn instead to worldly devices, like humor, drama, and other forms of entertainment.

Well, the world's methods may fill churches, just as they can fill stadiums for rock concerts, but work done in that way will be the world's work, not the work of God. This psalm tells us that if we would grow in grace and in the knowledge of God, be kept from sin, and be directed in a right path so that we will come into the presence of God in heaven at the last, we must be students of this Book. To use Francis Bacon's famous line, the Bible must be something we "read, mark, learn and inwardly digest."

The Bible meant more to the writer of this psalm than anything else in life. The psalm is his attempt to tell us why. If the Bible is equally precious to you, you will rejoice as you study this psalm and find yourself echoing the psalmist's statements in your own mind and heart. If the Bible is not precious to you, you should study this psalm to find out why it should be and perhaps come to love it as the psalmist did.

It was my privilege to expound this psalm to the congregation of Tenth Presbyterian Church of Philadelphia during the cold Northeast winter of 1996. As we studied the psalm together, we were spiritually warmed.

1
First Things First

Blessed are they whose ways are blameless,
  who walk according to the law of the LORD.
Blessed are they who keep his statutes
  and seek him with all their heart.
They do nothing wrong;
  they walk in his ways.
You have laid down precepts
  that are to be fully obeyed.
Oh, that my ways were steadfast
  in obeying your decrees!
Then I would not be put to shame
  when I consider all your commands.
I will praise you with an upright heart
  as I learn your righteous laws.
I will obey your decrees;
  do not utterly forsake me.

Psalm 119:1–8

AN ENTIRE PSALM ABOUT THE BIBLE? WHAT A SURPRISING thing! But should it really be surprising? Not when we consider that the Bible is the greatest of all God's good gifts to us and one we must learn to appreciate. Psalm 119 will help us do that. That is its purpose, to tell us how wonderful the Bible is and to help us understand it. Psalm 119 is a very great psalm. Derek Kidner, an Old Testament scholar, calls Psalm 119 a "giant among the psalms," saying that it "shows the full flowering of that 'delight . . . in the law of the Lord,' which is described in Psalm 1, and gives its personal witness to the many-sided qualities of Scripture praised in Psalm 19."[1]

So much has been written on Psalm 119 that it is impossible to cite even a portion of the works. In his *Treasury of David* Charles Spurgeon has 349 pages on this psalm, virtually a book in itself. Charles Bridges, a Church of England evangelical in the last century, wrote 481 pages (Banner of Truth Trust edition). His book contains a sermon for each of the psalm's twenty-two stanzas and was issued in 1827 when Bridges was only thirty-three years old. Most impressive is the three volume work by Thomas Manton. Each volume is between 500 and 600 pages in length, for a total of 1,677 pages, and there are 190 long chapters in all.

There are many fascinating stories connected with this psalm. One of the most amusing concerns George Wishart, a bishop of Edinburgh in the seventeenth century.[2] Wishart was condemned to death along with his famous patron, the Marquis of Montrose, and he would have been executed, except for this incident. When he was on the scaffold, he made use of a custom of the times that permitted the condemned to choose a psalm to be sung. He chose Psalm 119. Before two-thirds of the psalm was sung, a pardon arrived, and Wishart's life was spared. The story has been told as an illustration of God's intervention to save a saintly person. But the truth is actually different. Wishart was more renowned for shrewdness than for sanctity. He was expecting a pardon, requested the psalm to gain time and, happily for him, succeeded in delaying the execution until his pardon came.[3]

Some General Observations

Psalm 119 is an acrostic psalm, the most elaborate in the Psalter.[4] It is divided into twenty-two stanzas, one for each letter of the Hebrew alphabet, and each verse of each stanza begins with one of these letters in sequence. Thus each of the first eight verses begins with the letter *aleph*, each of the next eight verses begins with the letter *beth*, and so on. The acrostic pattern is highlighted by subheads in some English versions of the Bible.

The closest parallel in the Bible to this pattern is chapter three of Lamentations. It is divided into twenty-two sections also, like Psalm 119, but each of its sections has only three verses.

The most striking feature of Psalm 119—one that every commentator mentions because it is so important to the psalm's theme—is that each verse of the psalm, with only a few exceptions, refers to the Word of God, the Bible. The Massoretes, the scribes who added vowel pointings to the original Hebrew consonantal text, said that the Word of God is referred to in every verse but verse 122. Derek Kidner claims that there are three exceptions, verses 84, 121, and 122. Kidner seems to be right about verse 84, but verse 121 may not be an exception, if "righteous and just" can be understood as an oblique reference to God's Word. On the other hand, verses 90 and 132 also fail to mention the Bible, unless "faithfulness" in verse 90 and "name" in verse 132 mean God's Word. Whatever the case, at least 171 of the Psalm's 176 verses refer explicitly to the precepts, word, laws, commandments, or decrees of God.

This brings us to the synonyms for *Scripture* that dominate this psalm. There are at least eight of them that occur again and again: "law" *(torah)*, which occurs twenty-five times; "word" *(dabar)*, twenty-four times; "rulings" or "ordinances" *(mispatim)*, twenty-three times; "testimonies" *('edot)*, twenty-three times; "commandments" *(miswot)*, twenty-two times; "decrees" or "statutes" *(huqqim)*, twenty-one times; "precepts" or "charges" *(piqqudim)*, twenty-one times; and "sayings," "promise," or "word" *(ʾimrah)*, nineteen times. Other terms are close to being synonyms for Scripture, such as "way" (in verses 3, 15, and 30), and I have already mentioned the possibility that "righteous and just" and "name" mean the Bible. The rabbis said that there are ten synonyms for the Scriptures in this psalm, one for each of the Ten Commandments.

How to Be Blessed or Happy

Derek Kidner's reference to Psalm 119 as "the full flowering of that 'delight . . . in the law of the Lord' which is described in Psalm 1" is a happy reference on Kidner's part, because Psalm 119 begins like Psalm 1, by pronouncing a blessing on the one who forms his or her life according to the Word of God. Psalm 1 says,

> Blessed is the man [whose] . . .
>   delight is in the law of the LORD
>   verses 1–2

Psalm 119 begins with the same thought. There is a sense in which Psalm 119 is the Bible's most thorough exposition of the beatitude of Psalm 1, as seen in its opening lines:

> Blessed are they whose ways are blameless,
>   who walk according to the law of the LORD.
> Blessed are they who keep his statutes
>   and seek him with all their heart.
>   Psalm 119:1–2

Many writers acknowledge that to be happy is a universal goal of men and women. The only people who do not want to be happy are abnormal. But apart from being instructed by God, human beings do not know how to achieve happiness. They think they will be happy if they can earn enough money, be respected by those with whom they work, acquire enough power to do whatever they like or to be free from all restraints, or discover someone who will love them without conditions. But these pursuits do not ensure happiness, and sin always warps and destroys even the best achievements.

How can a person find happiness? The Bible tells us that the path to a happy life—the Bible's word for it is *blessedness*—is conforming to the law of God.

Here I must say something about the words that are used for God's law in this psalm. When we hear the word *law* we think of the kind of laws that are made by local, state, and federal legislatures, things like tax laws, environmental laws, traffic laws, and scores of other kinds of laws. These laws are intended for our good but they are essentially restrictive and, for the most part, we react negatively to them. There are laws like that in the Bible, of course: "You shall not murder," "You shall not commit adultery," "You shall not steal," and so on. But generally when the Bible speaks of the "law" *(torah)* of God, it has something much bigger in mind. It is referring to the whole of God's spoken and written revelation, containing all the various elements that the other words for law in this psalm suggest, including "words," "testimonies," "charges," "promises," and "ways."

We will look at each of those terms in detail as we go along, but here it is enough to say that what is being commended to us at the start of Psalm 119 is getting to know and live by the whole of God's revelation, which is what we call the Bible.

I stress living by the Bible, because that is what these opening verses emphasize. This is because the blessedness they speak of is for those who "walk" according to God's law and "keep" his statutes. In other words, from the beginning we are to understand that this is a practical matter, a way of life, and not merely a course of academic study. On the other hand, it is also clear that we cannot live by the Bible unless we know it well. As the first psalm says, it must be our "meditat[ion] day and night" (v. 2).

I suggest that if we are to meditate on the Bible day and night, we must have at least some if it committed to memory, which is what Christians in past ages of the church did. Several years ago when I was preaching on Psalm 117, I suggested that it should be memorized. It is a short psalm and a few people memorized it. But in the past it was not uncommon for people to memorize Psalm 119, the longest chapter in the Bible.

John Ruskin was not a minister or even a theologian. He lived in the nineteenth century and was a British writer who specialized in works of art criticism. But he had been raised by a Calvinistic mother who was unsparing both of herself and others and who, in his youth, had made him memorize large portions of the Bible. He memorized Psalms 23, 32, 90, 91, 103, 112, 119, and 139, to give just some examples. Later in his life Ruskin wrote of Psalm 119, "It is strange that of all the pieces of the Bible which my mother taught me, that which cost me most to learn, and which was, to my childish mind, chiefly repulsive—the 119th Psalm—has now become of all the most precious to me in its overflowing and glorious passion of love for the Law of God."[5]

William Wilberforce, the British statesman who was largely responsible for the abolition of the slave trade throughout the empire, wrote in his diary in the year 1819, "Walked today from Hyde Park Corner, repeating the 119th Psalm in great comfort."[6]

Does it seem strange that busy Wilberforce should know this psalm by heart? Perhaps. But here are two others who memorized it.

Henry Martyn, that great pioneer missionary to India, memorized Psalm 119 as an adult in 1804. He had an extremely arduous life, but he confessed that it was the Bible alone that gave him strength to keep going. He died of exhaustion from his missionary efforts in 1812.

David Livingstone, the great pioneer missionary to Africa, won a Bible from his Sunday school teacher by repeating Psalm 119 by heart—when he was only nine years old.

Each of these persons achieved a great deal for God. And who is to say that it was not their personal, word-by-word knowledge of the Bible that enabled them not only to live a godly life but also to accomplish what they did?

I think of Derrick Bingham, a powerful Irish lay preacher whom I had the privilege of meeting in the summer of 1986 when I was in England taking part in the great Keswick convention. He told how he was called to the ministry through his mother. Every Irishman has a deathbed story about his dying mother, it seems, and Derrick is no exception. He told me that as his mother was dying, she said to him, "Derrick, my boy, you have the gift of gab. But you don't know the Word. If you'd learn the Word, the Lord might be able to use you." Derrick took that to heart, determined to study the Bible, and within three weeks of his mother's death he was preaching.

We are not all called to be preachers, of course. But I am sure we could accomplish a great deal more of spiritual value than we do if we would only determine to get to know the Bible as John Ruskin, William Wilberforce, Henry Martyn, David Livingstone, and Derrick Bingham did. But we don't. Instead we allow ourselves to be taken captive by the patterns of this world and fill our heads with its passing idle pleasures and fantasies.

Knowing and Obeying God's Word

But maybe I have said too much about *knowing* the Bible. The point of the opening verses of Psalm 119 is not merely that we must know the Bible, but that we must determine to live by it or, as we can also say, to keep it or obey it. This has already been stated in verses 1 and 2. But the point is made even stronger in verses 3 and 4:

They do nothing wrong;
they walk in his ways.
You have laid down precepts
that are to be fully obeyed.

The reason we are not happy is that we sin, and the main reason we sin as much as we do is that we do not know the Bible well enough. These verses tell us that the happy people are those who "do nothing wrong." However, if we ask how they have learned not to do wrong, the answer surely is that they have learned to "walk in [God's] ways" and "obey" his precepts.

The great Lutheran commentator on the psalms, H. C. Leupold, asks us to "note throughout [the psalm] how the law is sought for the very purpose of being kept, not for the sake of attaining a theoretical knowledge of it."[7] This is a truth taught elsewhere in the Bible, of course, but it is very apparent in Psalm 119. Notice the words referring to human response and responsibility in just this first stanza: walk, keep, obey, and learn. We will see them again, as well as other similar terms, as we go on.

An Honest Wish

Sometimes when we read the Bible we get the idea that its characters were special people very unlike ourselves. We are only beginning our study of this psalm and already we read about those people who are happy because they live blamelessly according to the law of the Lord, keep his statutes, and seek him with their whole heart. The psalmist must be one of these very blessed people, we think. Otherwise he would not be writing as he does. However, we do not get very far into the psalm before we discover that he is very much like us in that he is not yet like the happy, blessed ones he is describing. He wants to be, but he is not there yet. Therefore, he cries, "Oh, that my ways were steadfast in obeying your decrees!" (v. 5).

There is something that rings true and is commendably honest about this heartfelt cry of the psalmist. He is a very godly man, but it almost seems contradictory that he is acutely aware of how ungodly he still is.

I think he is saying in this verse almost exactly what the apostle Paul wrote at much greater length in Romans 7:

> I do not understand what I do. For what I want to do I do not do, but what I hate I do. . . . I have the desire to do what is good, but I cannot carry it out. For what I do is not the good I want to do; no, the evil I do not want to do— this I keep on doing. . . . So I find this law at work: When I want to do good, evil is right there with me. For in my inner being I delight in God's law; but I see another law at work in the members of my body, waging war against the law of my mind and making me a prisoner of the law of sin at work within my members.
>
> Romans 7:15, 18–19, 21–23

Some people who have written on Romans 7 have supposed that in these verses Paul is writing about himself as an unbeliever, that is, before he came to know Jesus Christ as his Savior. But that is not the case at all. Paul is writing as a Christian, saying that life even for an apostle is a struggle. Although we want to keep the law of God, we do not keep it and, in fact, cannot keep it, at least not in our own power. Paul's statement is a case of what J. I. Packer calls "spiritual realism,"[8] mere honesty before the living God.

But honesty is not the whole story. The psalmist has not yet attained the obedience for which he yearns. He admits this openly. But it is possible to admit many things honestly and never go beyond the honesty, never make any progress toward a better or more obedient way of life. This is not the case for the psalmist. He wants to make progress. So the question for us now is not so much: Is the psalmist like us? Instead it is: Are we like him? Are we like him in his desire to seek God, know the Bible, and actually obey God's commands?

A Strong Resolution

How determined was the psalmist to obey God? For an answer I take you to the last verse of the stanza—his determined resolution: "I will obey your decrees; do not utterly forsake me" (v. 8). This verse is at one and the same time a strong resolution, a sincere confession, and an urgent plea. The resolution: I am resolved to obey God's decrees. The confession: I cannot obey God's decrees unless God enables me to do so. The plea: Therefore, do not forsake me, O my God. This does not mean that the psalmist thinks God might somehow abandon him in the matter of his salvation. He was as aware as we should be that God's calling is unalterable. God has said, "Never will I leave you; never will I forsake you" (Heb. 13:5; see Deut. 31:6). The psalmist is asking God to stick by him in his determination to live according to God's law.

This first stanza has moved from statements about the Bible as a source of blessing for all persons to a very personal resolution. If the psalm is to be helpful to us, it must become personal in our lives too.

2

Starting Young

How can a young man keep his way pure?
　　By living according to your word.
I seek you with all my heart;
　　do not let me stray from your commands.
I have hidden your word in my heart
　　that I might not sin against you.
Praise be to you, O LORD;
　　teach me your decrees.
With my lips I recount
　　all the laws that come from your mouth.
I rejoice in following your statutes
　　as one rejoices in great riches.
I meditate on your precepts
　　and consider your ways.
I delight in your decrees;
　　I will not neglect your word.

Psalm 119:9–16

EACH VERSE OF THE SECOND STANZA OF PSALM 119 BEGINS
with the Hebrew letter *beth*. The interesting thing about *beth*
is that the word also means "a house," and the importance of
this point, as Herbert Lockyer notes, is that the underlying

thought of the stanza is that of "making our heart a home for the Word of God."[1]

What is the condition of your heart? Apart from the grace of God in your life, it will always be occupied by such filthy evil spirits as lust, greed, pride, and self-love. If you try to exorcise these demons by yourself, they will only return in greater numbers and your latter state will be worse than at the first (Luke 11:24–26). God alone can cleanse the heart, and he does it through the agency of his Word, the Bible. "How can a young man keep his way pure?" Answer: "By living according to your word."

> How can a young man keep his way pure?
>   By living according to your word.
> I seek you with all my heart;
>   do not let me stray from your commands.
> I have hidden your word in my heart
>   that I might not sin against you.
>
> verses 9–11

When Should We Begin?

So then, in order to live a holy life we must give ourselves to God's Word—learning it and living by it. But when should we start to do this? The world has its answer. It says, Have your fling when you are young and settle down to being religious when you get old, if then. God's answer is quite different. God says, If you are going to live for me, you must begin at the earliest possible moment, without delay, preferably when you are very young (v. 9). If you do not live for me when you are young, you will probably not live for me when you are older either, and the end of your life will be ruinous.[2]

It does not require a great deal of wisdom to see why this is such good advice and so necessary. It is because the decisions of youth form habits that guide us from that point forward and are hard to break. If we form good habits when we are young—reading the Bible, spending time in prayer, enjoying the company of God's people, going to church, rejecting sin, practicing honesty, and doing good—these patterns will go with us through life and make it easier to choose good later in life. If, on the contrary, we make bad choices, later we will find good choices harder to make and the bad habits nearly impossible to break.

This point is so important that the Bible gives us numerous examples of young men who chose God's way early in life and were blessed for it. Daniel and his three young friends are examples. When they were taken from their home in Jerusalem and brought to Babylon to serve the court of King Nebuchadnezzar, they were given the best of the food of Babylon, as favored civil servants. But we read in Daniel 1:8: "Daniel resolved not to defile himself with the royal food and wine."

This was the first of many tests that came into Daniel's life during his lengthy career in Babylon, and it established a pattern that enabled him to stand against the many traps later laid by his enemies. To us, whether or not he would eat the king's food or drink his wine seems a small matter, hardly something to be fussed over. We don't follow kosher rules, and most of us care very little about our diet. Choosing what we eat is not a major concern. Yet that is just the point. It is the small things that form habits and it is our habits that determine the course and outcome of our lives.

Years ago when I was studying Daniel, I wrote,

Are you a young person? Then you should pay particularly close attention to this point. Most young people want their lives to count, and most Christian young people want their lives to count for God. Youth dreams big. That is right. You should dream big. But youth is also often impatient and undisciplined, and young people are tempted to let the little things slide. You must not do that if you are God's young man or God's young woman. God will make your life count, but this will not happen unless you determine to live for him in the little things now.[3]

This section of Psalm 119 is telling us that the best possible way to live for God and establish and maintain a pure life is to start young.

In his last will and testament, the Protestant Reformer Theodore Beza thanked God for the mercy of having been called to the knowledge of the truth when he was a youth of sixteen and thus, during a course of more than seventy years of walking with God, of having escaped "the pollutions of the world through lust."[4]

What Should We Do?

The first three verses of this section of Psalm 119 not only tell us that we should begin to live for God early in life—or, in case we are already older, at the earliest possible moment, that is, right now—they also tell us what we should actually do to live for God. We must hide God's word in our hearts. This doesn't mean just reading it but also studying it and even memorizing it. In fact memorizing is precisely what is called for, since it is only when the Word of God is readily available in our minds that we are able to recall it in moments of need and to profit by it.

This point is closely tied to starting young, for it is far easier to memorize and retain material when a person is young than when he or she is older. Here is one of the great failures of the contemporary church. Because children and other young people can memorize easily, churches should stress memorization for those in their early years. But instead of doing this, many churches, along with the general culture, have been "dumbing down" Christian education so that children today are taught barely anything in these vital early years. Instead of solid biblical theology, Bible memorization, and great hymns, they are offered trivial stories, pointless games, and banal songs.

Years ago we determined to resist this trend at Tenth Presbyterian Church in Philadelphia, where I serve as senior minister. Shortly after I began my pastorate in the late 1960s, a number of interested people put together a Sunday school curriculum in which the emphasis is on the great truths of the Bible, taught in three-year cycles. The first year teaches these great truths as a sequence of important doctrines. The second year approaches the same truths in terms of a person's relationship to God and other people. The third year looks at these same teachings from the standpoint of history, asking, What is God doing in history? and How do I fit in? The curriculum repeats this cycle every three years, so there is a constant reinforcement of these truths among the young people.

Together with this curriculum we outlined a thorough Bible memorization program in which parts of verses are learned by the youngest students, whole verses and short passages by older children, and eventually even several long chapters by those who are coming to the end of their Bible school years. We also have the children memorize a simplified catechism, based on the Westminster Shorter Catechism. And we teach them some of the great hymns of the church instead of choruses.

Does it work? We know that the regenerating work of the Spirit of God in human hearts cannot be accomplished through any amount of good teaching. Regeneration and growth are the work of God, not the work of man. But since it is only through the saving revelation of God in Scripture that God himself may be found, teaching the great truths of Scripture is essential. We should notice that in these first three verses of this psalm section the psalmist links pursuit of God's Word to the pursuit of God himself. "I seek you with all my heart" (v. 10). Therefore, I live "according to your word" (v. 9).

Why Should We Do It?

Thus far we have seen that we must begin to study the Bible when we are young or, at any rate, at the earliest possible moment, and that we must proceed by memorizing the

Word to hide it in our hearts and have it readily available. Why should we make such an effort? We have seen one answer already; it is that we might get to know God. But what the poet is particularly interested in here is that we might live holy lives, that is, that we might not sin against God (v. 11).

We live in a corrupt and sinful world, and there is nothing in the world that in itself will help us live a pure life. More than one hundred years ago the highly respected Bible teacher Alexander Maclaren wrote that the world is

> a great deal fuller of inducements to do wrong than of inducements to do right, . . . a great many bad things that have a deceptive appearance of pleasure, a great many circumstances in which it seems far easier to follow the worse than to follow the better course. And so unless a man has learned the great art of saying, "No!" "So did not I because of the fear of the Lord," he will come to rack and ruin without a doubt.[5]

What can preserve us from ruin? What can empower us to say no to temptation? What can enable us to live a holy life in the midst of our most wicked surroundings? Only the Word of God, the Bible, which we must study and hide away in our hearts. Jesus told his disciples, "You are already clean *because of the word* I have spoken to you" (John 15:3, italics mine). He also prayed to the Father on their behalf, saying, "Sanctify them *by the truth*," noting that *"your word is truth"* (John 17:17, italics mine).

Here is an outline for verse 11 that may help you remember what we have noticed in the psalm thus far:

> The best thing—"thy Word"
> Hidden in the best place—"my heart"
> For the best purpose—"that I might not sin against thee"[6]

Remember that the Bible is God's cleansing agent for sin and that without it you will never live a holy life.

The Divine Teacher

There is a fourth important teaching in this stanza. We cannot understand God's Word by ourselves, and therefore we need God himself for our teacher. Verse 12 notes this by coupling a line of praise with a line of petition: "Praise be to you, O LORD; teach me your decrees."

The Protestant Reformers had an important way of talking about this truth. They stressed the necessary link between God's Word and God's Spirit. These men—Martin Luther, John Calvin, and others—had a very strong trust in the Bible. They recognized that although God has revealed himself in a general way in creation so that people are without excuse if they fail to seek him out and thank him for life and its blessings, and although he has also revealed himself preeminently in Jesus Christ, the only place we have saving revelation and the only way we can know about Jesus is in the Bible. They understood that the only way we can get to know God is through God's self-revelation in his written Word.

At the same time they were also aware that if we are to understand and rightly apply the Bible, we need the Holy Spirit to teach us. They thought of such verses as 1 John 5:6: "The Spirit . . . testifies, because the Spirit is the truth." Or 1 Corinthians 2:12–14:

> We have not received the spirit of the world but the Spirit who is from God, that we may understand what God has freely given us. This is what we speak, not in words taught us by human wisdom but in words taught by the Spirit, expressing spiritual truths in spiritual words. The man without the Spirit does not accept the things that come from the Spirit of God, for they are foolishness to him, and he cannot understand them, because they are spiritually discerned.

When Luther, Calvin, and the others thought of these verses that stress the work of the Holy Spirit, they understood that although we have the Bible to study, we must also have the Holy Spirit to help us understand what is taught in it. They said that without the Spirit the Bible is a dead book. That is why the man "without the Spirit" cannot understand it. On the other hand, without the Word as an objective guide from God, claims to a special leading by the Holy Spirit lead to error, excess, or foolishness.

This means that when we study the Bible we must also pray, asking God to be our teacher. For it is God himself we are seeking after all, and his thoughts are not our thoughts, neither are his ways our ways (Isa. 55:8). Besides, our sinful and deceitful hearts will keep us from hearing and obeying God unless God himself breaks through to teach us.

Four Helpful Exercises

So where do we go from here? What are some practical steps we might take to get the Bible into our minds and hearts and begin to make progress in the Christian life? The psalmist seems to be writing primarily to the young in this stanza, so it is not surprising to find him ending with four points of very practical advice, expressed in terms of his own experience. We might call them four exercises for mastering Scripture. We should practice each one.

1. *"With my lips I recount all the laws that come from your mouth"* (v. 13). One of the best ways to learn anything is to verbalize it or teach it to others. I find that I have a far easier time learning some truth and I retain it longer if I work it into a sermon or make it part of one of our Bible study seminars.

Not long ago I attended a meeting of the board of directors of Bible Study Fellowship and learned about an African woman who attends one of the large classes in Nairobi. Each week, after attending the Nairobi class, she goes back to her village and teaches what she has learned to about forty women who gather to hear her. Who do you think learns most from the Nairobi class? And who will retain it longest? If we are alive for God, our lives will be like the muscle of the heart that is constantly expanding to take in a fresh supply of blood, which is the life, and then contracting to push it on and give it out.

And speaking of the heart, Martin Luther observed that some people speak God's truth but do not have it in their hearts, while others have it in their hearts but are afraid to proclaim it vigorously for fear of losing friends and making enemies and persecutors. He said, "It is not enough to believe with the heart unto righteousness, unless confession unto salvation is also made with the mouth" (Rom. 10:10).[7]

2. *"I rejoice in following your statutes"* (v. 14). It is a natural tendency of a healthy mind to remember things that are pleasant and forget things that are unpleasant. A person who does the opposite is mentally or psychologically unstable. It follows from this that one good way to learn and retain God's Word is to rejoice in it, as the psalmist says he does. That can be done in a lot of ways, privately in our personal devotions and publicly in witnessing situations. Let me suggest that one very excellent way is by joyful worship in regular church services. I am seldom more joyful than when I am singing the great hymns of the faith in church with other Christians.

3. *"I meditate on your precepts"* (v. 15). The third thing the writer of this psalm commends to us is meditation. That is, recalling what we have committed to memory and then turning it over and over in our minds to see the fullest implications and applications of the truth. The Virgin Mary did this after the birth of her son, the Lord Jesus Christ, for we are told in Luke 2:19, "But Mary treasured up all these things and pondered them in her heart."

4. *"I delight in your decrees; I will not neglect your word"* (v. 16). The psalmist's final point of practical advice is to determine never to neglect God's word. "Delight" in this last verse is not the same word as in verse 14 ("rejoice"). "Rejoice" refers to an exuberant festive joyfulness. "Delight" is a settled pleasure. The two are expressions of the same emotion, but "delight," in the last line, is used along with a de-

termination not to neglect Bible study. If we delight in God's Word we won't neglect it. We will determine not to allow other pressing matters to crowd out our Bible study.

Did you notice the future tense ("I will") in that last line? In some translations the future tense of verbs is used in earlier verses. But according to the New International Version, it is here that the author changes from declaring what he has done or is in the habit of doing to what he will do. Here he determines not to neglect the Bible but to study it faithfully.

3
Trials on the Way

Do good to your servant, and I will live;
   I will obey your word.
Open my eyes that I may see
   wonderful things in your law.
I am a stranger on earth;
   do not hide your commands from me.
My soul is consumed with longing
   for your laws at all times.
You rebuke the arrogant, who are cursed
   and who stray from your commands.
Remove from me scorn and contempt,
   for I keep your statutes.
Though rulers sit together and slander me,
   your servant will meditate on your decrees.
Your statutes are my delight;
   they are my counselors.

I am laid low in the dust;
   preserve my life according to your word.
I recounted my ways and you answered me;
   teach me your decrees.
Let me understand the teaching of your precepts;

then I will meditate on your wonders.
My soul is weary with sorrow;
strengthen me according to your word.
Keep me from deceitful ways;
be gracious to me through your law.
I have chosen the way of truth;
I have set my heart on your laws.
I hold fast to your statutes, O LORD;
do not let me be put to shame.
I run in the path of your commands,
for you have set my heart free.

Psalm 119:17–32

E. M. BLAIKLOCK IS A WELL-KNOWN BIBLE SCHOLAR FROM Australia and a former professor of classics at the University of Auckland, New Zealand. He has written *The Bible & I* about the influence of the Bible on his life.[1] At one point in his book he thinks back over the weeks he once spent lecturing on Psalm 119 and how, as he studied and lectured, he came to appreciate the suffering the writer seems to have gone through.

Here is how he writes about the psalm's author.

He had known persecution, that most hideous of man's sins (22, 23); he had suffered under the heavy or the ruthless hand of authority, as Christians (and Jews) still do in the lands where the blanket of the dark has fallen (61, 69). His faith had staggered under the load of it all (6, 22, 31). He had known pressure to give in and conform. . . . The third section [which, along with the fourth, is the subject of this chapter] seems to be particularly autobiographical. The writer had known deprivation and fear for his life (17), the dryness of soul of which Cowper wrote ("where is the blessedness I knew . . .") when the word itself seems to lose its savor (18) under the stress of life. He had known loneliness and rejection (19) [and] the agony of seeming abandonment (20).

As Blaiklock worked through these prayers and expressions, a man seemed to emerge through the mist of words whom, he said, he seemed both "to know and understand."[2] I want to suggest that the psalmist is a person we too should know and understand, simply because he is so much like us—at least in these experiences.

For Righteousness Sake

There are many references throughout the psalm to the trials the writer had gone through, as Blaiklock's overview indicates. We will see more of them in the three sections comprising verses 65–88 *(teth, yodh,* and *kaph)*. But here in verses 17–32 there are examples of trials as well, and what is unique about these specific trials is that they seem to have come to the psalmist because of his determination to adhere to God's Word. In other words, it is not just the trials and tribulations common to mankind that we are looking at in the stanzas marked *gimel* and *daleth,* but rather those trials that come to a person when he or she is being persecuted for the sake of righteousness (see Matt. 5:10).

This fits together well with what the writer has been saying thus far in the psalm. He began, in the first stanza, by speaking of the blessedness that comes to the person who determines to live according to the law of God. In the second stanza he suggests that the time to start living by God's law is when a person is young. Now, in stanzas three and four, he speaks of the trials that will come to one who is walking in that way. These seem to fall into four categories: alienation, slander, abasement, and sorrow.

Alienation

The psalmist's feelings of alienation are reflected in his words, "I am a stranger on earth" (v. 19). There are two ideas here. First, the words suggest that we are only passing through this world for a short while with but little time to know and live by God's Word. Therefore, we should devote ourselves to getting to know the Bible. The psalmist seems to be saying that since he is "a stranger on earth" he wants to spend all the time he can in God's Word: "Do not hide your commands from me" and "my soul is consumed with longing for your laws at all times." The idea would be similar to the rhyme we sometimes hear:

> Only one life, it will soon be past.
> Only what's done for Christ will last.

In this case the concern of the psalmist is with getting to know and then actually live by God's Word.

The second idea connected with alienation is that of being out of place in this world. Believers are alienated from the world because they belong to God, whom the world does not know or honor. This thought seems to be supported by the larger context, for after speaking of his own desire to know God's commands, the poet writes of the "arrogant, who are cursed and who stray from your commands" (v. 21) and the "rulers" who "sit together and slander me" (v. 23).

It is important to know and come to terms with the fact that if you are trying to follow God, the world is going to treat you as an alien, for that is what you are. You cannot expect to be at home here, and if you are, well, that is an indication that you really do not belong to Christ or at least are living far from him. Do you think that is too harsh? Jesus expressed it in even stronger terms.

> If you belonged to the world, it would love you as its own. As it is, you do not belong to the world, but I have chosen you out of the world. That is why the world hates you. Remember the words I spoke to you: "No servant is greater than his master." If they persecuted me, they will persecute you also.
>
> John 15:19–20

We may not be at home in a world that does not know God but we have a home in God and can rejoice in him because he alone is finally satisfying. Saint Augustine said it well: "Thou hast formed us for thyself, and our hearts are restless till they find rest in thee."[3]

Slander

The psalmist experienced alienation, partly because of the slander directed against him by the rulers (vv. 22–23). We have seen that believers feel like "strangers on earth" because they really are strangers. They do not fit in. That is an accurate description of their condition. But slander is another matter. Slander is not accurate. It is by definition untrue. It has to do with assigning false motives to the good we may be trying to do and even charging us with evil that we do not do. Not to fit in often seems bad enough. But to be falsely accused when we are actually trying to live for God and do good is worse. Yet that is what many believers experience.

Alexander Maclaren wrote how this slander results from the writer's determination to live by God's law.

> The last three verses of the section appear to be linked together. They relate to the persecutions of the psalmist for his faithfulness to God's law. In verse 22 he prays that reproach and shame, which wrapped him like a covering, may be lifted from him; and his plea in verse 22b declares that he lay under these because he was true to God's statutes. In verse 23 we see the source of the reproach and shame, in the conclave of men in authority, whether foreign princes or Jewish rulers, who were busy slandering him, and plotting his ruin; while, with wonderful beauty, the contrasted picture [in verse 23b] shows the object of that busy talk, sitting silently absorbed in meditation on the higher things of God's statutes.[4]

When we are falsely accused, all we can do is take our cause to God, who will vindicate us in his own time. Meanwhile we must continue to study the Bible and try to live for God as best we can in this world.

Abasement or Humiliation

In the next stanza the writer gives two more examples of what he was suffering because he had determined to live according to God's Word. The first of these is abasement or humiliation, which he expresses as being "laid low in the dust" (v. 25). The Hebrew actually speaks of "cleaving" to the dust, that is, of being so low that one actually seems to be bonded to humiliation.

Sorrow

The fourth trial for the person seeking to walk according to the way of the Lord is grief. The writer says that his soul has been made "weary with sorrow" (v. 28). There are different things we feel sorrow about. We sorrow over the unregenerate world that is perishing. We sorrow for our own sins. We sorrow at the loss, either through death or by misunderstanding, of a person who has been close to us. But here the psalmist seems to be expressing sorrow because he has been rejected, slandered, and humiliated by other people.

Have you ever felt that way? Most of us at one time or another have felt terribly "down." There is nothing wrong with that in itself. It is a natural response to the kind of trials the psalmist has been describing. But it would be wrong to allow such feelings to turn us inward or, even worse, away from God. Instead of looking inward, the writer of Psalm 119 renews his determination to hold fast to the promises of God. His response is, "Strengthen me according to your word."

Living by God's Word

The trials the psalmist experienced added up to the threat of death or annihilation. But the psalmist wants to live. That is the point at which each of these two stanzas begins: "Do good to your servant, and I will live. . . . preserve my life according to your word" (vv. 17, 25).

It is not mere physical life that he wants, however. What he really wants is the fullness of spiritual life. Hence, his concern is to live by the Word of God. He says that he is "consumed with longing" for it (v. 20), that it is his "delight" (v. 24), that he has "chosen the way of truth" (v. 30), and that he wants to "hold fast to [God's] statutes" (v. 31).

The writer of this psalm lived hundreds of years before Jesus Christ but if he had been living in Christ's day, he would have understood readily Jesus' reply to the first of the devil's temptations. Jesus had been led into a wilderness area by God's Spirit and after having fasted for forty days, he was hungry. The devil came to him suggesting, "If you are the Son of God, tell these stones to become bread" (Matt. 4:3).

Jesus replied, "It is written: 'Man does not live on bread alone, but on every word that comes from the mouth of God,'" quoting from Deuteronomy 8:3 (Matt. 4:4). He meant that it is more important to feed spiritually on God's Word than to feed on physical food. Likewise, the psalmist knew that it was more important for him to meditate on God's decrees and obey them than to escape the world's contempt and hatred, if escaping that hatred meant turning his back on God's Word.

Wonderful Things in God's Law

In each of the stanzas we have studied thus far we have found the writer's confession that although he has determined to study God's Word and live by it, he nevertheless cannot do this by himself. In the first stanza he cried out, "I will obey your decrees; do not utterly forsake me" (v. 8). In the second stanza he prayed, "Teach me your decrees" (v. 12). It is the same in stanzas three and four. Here he is reflecting on the many trials that have come to him because he wants to live by

God's law. Still if he is going to be able to live by it, God will have to open it up to him, teach him, give him understanding, and keep him from other, false ways. He prays for four things.

1. *"Open my eyes"* (vv. 18–19). The verb *open* in verse 18 is used in the Balaam story in Numbers where the Lord opened Balaam's eyes so he could see the angel of the Lord standing in the road with his sword drawn (Num. 22:31). It has to do with removing a veil or covering. Here it does not mean that the Word itself is covered, as if it were somehow unclear. The Bible is perfectly clear. That is what we mean when we speak of the clarity or perspicuity of Scripture, a subject we are going to be looking at closely in chapter 9. There is nothing obscure about the Bible. Rather, the obscurity is in us. Therefore what we need is the removing of the veil from our eyes so we can see those "wonderful things" that are in Scripture.

Howard Carter was the world-renowned Egyptologist who, in 1922, discovered the marvelous gold artifacts in the tomb of King Tutankhamen. After he had exposed the steps leading down to the burial chamber, Carter summoned Lord Carnarvon, the expedition's sponsor, to be present when the tomb was opened. The two men made their way down the steps and had the workmen push back the last covering over the door of the entrance chamber. Lord Carnarvon asked impatiently, "Do you see anything?"

"Yes, wonderful things" was Carter's memorable answer.

And wonderful they were—the most lavish, most beautiful objects ever found in any ancient tomb! Still they pale when compared with the far more wonderful things to be found in Scripture when God opens a person's spiritually blind eyes to perceive them. The treasures in Scripture are wonderful in themselves, wonderful because their source is in God, wonderful because of what they do in us and for us, and wonderful because they are everlasting when everything else we know is rapidly passing away.

Do you remember the two Emmaus disciples? Jesus opened their eyes to see how he had to suffer and then enter into his glory. Afterward they testified, "Were not our hearts burning within us while he talked with us on the road and opened the Scriptures to us?" (Luke 24:32).

God must open our eyes, but that is not the whole story. For while he was praying, the psalmist was doing his part, which he describes in verses 20 and following as: first, "longing for your laws" (v. 20); second, "meditat[ing] on your decrees" (v. 23); and third, "delight[ing]" in God's statutes (v. 24).

In the *Treasury of David* Charles Haddon Spurgeon cites John Kerr as writing, "A man will never grow into the knowledge of God's word by idly waiting for some new gift of discernment, but by diligently using that which God has already bestowed upon him, and using at the same time all other helps that lie within his reach."[5] In other words, if we want to see wonderful things in the Scriptures, it is not enough for us merely to ask God to open our eyes that we might see them. We must also carefully study the Bible. The Holy Spirit is given not to make our study unnecessary but to make it effective.

2. *"Teach me your decrees"* (v. 26). The second thing the psalmist prays for is that God would teach him his decrees. This is the same request he made in stanza two, verse 12. Remember the teaching of the Protestant Reformers who always stressed that the written Word of God and the activity of the Spirit of God go together. The Spirit speaks through the Word. So if we desire to grow in grace, we need both to study the Bible and to ask God through his Holy Spirit to be our teacher.

3. *"Let me understand the teaching"* (v. 27). In verse 26 the writer says, "Teach me your decrees," and then in verse 27 he adds, "Let me understand the teaching of your precepts." This could be another instance of parallelism so common in Hebrew poetry. But it is probably more than this, since the second verse goes on to speak of meditating on the Bible's wonders. In other words, this is a reference to a deep understanding, one that goes beyond a mere perception of the words'

meanings to a profound understanding of what they reveal about the nature of God, the gospel, and God's ways.

4. *"Keep me from deceitful ways"* (v. 29). The last of the psalmist's four requests is that he might be kept from sin, which is what he has been thinking about all along. We are kept from sin by the grace of God, of course, but the verse is more specific than this. It is by the grace of God, being exercised through the written word. Verse 29 makes this point more strongly in the Hebrew text than in English, since the single verb translated "be gracious" in our text actually has the sense of "graciously teach." The full thought is: If we are to be kept from sin, it must be by the grace of God through the teaching of his Word. We saw this earlier: "How can a young man keep his way pure?" Answer: "By living according to your word" (v. 9).

Running the Race

We have already seen in the third stanza that, although God must be our teacher, there are nevertheless things we need to do: "long for" God's laws (v. 20), "meditate" on his decrees (v. 23), and "delight" in his statutes (v. 24). It is the same as we come to the end of stanza four. Here, in the last three verses, the psalmist indicates by three powerful verbs—choose, hold fast, and run—what else is required if we are to live a godly life.

1. *We must choose the right way* (v. 30). Nobody ever just stumbles onto the right path. We can stumble away from it. But if we are going to live for God by learning and obeying his Word, the Bible, we must choose to do so and apply ourselves firmly to the task. The psalmist indicates the nature of his choice when he says, "I have chosen the way of truth; I have set my heart on your laws."

2. *We must hold God's statutes fast* (v. 31). *Hold* is the same word as *laid low* in verse 25. Literally it means "to cleave."

In verse 25 the psalmist said he was cleaving to the dust, so great was his humiliation; here he is found cleaving to God's Word. Would this were the case with each of us, that is, that the result of our being struck down and humbled would be that we likewise would commit ourselves to God's Word. We may be struck down, but in our abasement we need to hold the Word high. Indeed, what else is there to do? In times of acute distress there is nothing to cleave to but God and his testimonies. It was said of Moses that he spent forty years in the wilderness learning to be nothing so that he might spend the next forty years proving God to be everything.

3. *We must run the course set before us* (v. 32). This fourth stanza began by the psalmist being "laid low." But here at the end he is running vigorously and freely in God's way. Do you see your Christian life as a race to be won? Or do you regard it merely as a casual stroll? Do you follow your Lord apathetically and at a distance? Hebrews 12:1 urges,

> Let us throw off everything that hinders and the sin that so easily entangles, and let us run with perseverance the race marked out for us.

Likewise, the apostle Paul declared,

> I have fought the good fight, I have finished the race, I have kept the faith. Now there is in store for me the crown of righteousness, which the Lord, the righteous Judge, will award to me on that day—and not only to me, but also to all who have longed for his appearing.
>
> 2 Timothy 4:7–8

4

In God's School

Teach me, O LORD, to follow your decrees;
  then I will keep them to the end.
Give me understanding, and I will keep your law
  and obey it with all my heart.
Direct me in the path of your commands,
  for there I find delight.
Turn my heart toward your statutes
  and not toward selfish gain.
Turn my eyes away from worthless things;
  preserve my life according to your word.
Fulfill your promise to your servant,
  so that you may be feared.
Take away the disgrace I dread,
  for your laws are good.
How I long for your precepts!
  Preserve my life in your righteousness.
                                    Psalm 119:33–40

CHRISTIANITY AND LEARNING HAVE ALWAYS GONE HAND IN hand. Wherever the gospel of Jesus Christ has gone in this world, grammar schools, literacy classes, scholarship, and schools of higher learning have inevitably followed its advance. This is because the gospel opens the mind not only to matters of the soul, but to the mind itself, to nature, man, history, and the marvels of the world God created. In the fifth stanza of Psalm 119 we have this important combination: learning and religion. But the kind of learning the psalmist has in mind is learning God's Word. Moreover, he wants to learn God's Word so he can walk in it or obey it. To make progress in this school, he asks God to be his teacher.

This stanza is filled with prayers, nine in all. There is a linguistic reason for the prayers. As Leslie Allen points out, this is the fifth or *he* stanza of the psalm (*he* being the fifth letter of the Hebrew alphabet), and it is a characteristic of Hebrew that *he* is used at the beginning of verbs to make them causative.[1] In English we would translate such verbs as "Cause me to learn," "Cause me to have understanding," "Cause me to walk," and so on. This is awkward English, so the verbs are better rendered as petitions, which is what the Hebrew sentences actually are. As a result we have: "Teach me, O LORD, to follow your decrees" (v. 33); "Give me understanding" (v. 34); "Direct me in the path of your commands" (v. 35); "Turn my heart toward your statutes" (v. 36); and so on throughout the stanza.

Putting prayer and a desire to learn God's Word together then, what we have in the fifth stanza of Psalm 119 is a series of prayers for acceptance, progress, assistance, and perseverance in God's school of spiritual learning.

Matriculating in God's School

Often when a person is applying for admission to a university in this country, one of the questions on the application form will be: Why do you want to come to this university? Or, What do you hope to gain from a course of study at this institution? A clever student will write something along the line of, "I hope to become the well-rounded, intelligent, contributing person I know I can be, and that I believe only your school can make me." Or, "I think your institution is the best one to help me develop and employ my considerable talents."

In the first two verses of this stanza the author is doing something like this. That is, he is applying for matriculation in God's school. In his case, however, he is applying not because of what he has and wants to develop, but because of what he does not have but needs to acquire to live a holy life.

These verses ask God to "teach" him to follow God's decrees and "give . . . understanding" to keep God's law. These requests are virtually the same. The reason he is asking for instruction is because he desires to keep God's decrees "to the end" and to be able to obey God's law "with all my heart." "To the end" means without limit as to time, and "with all my heart" means without reservation on his part. The writer is asking for two things that he lacks: understanding and the ability to do what he understands.

Charles Bridges observed this: "We are equally ignorant of the path of God's commandments, and impotent to go in it. We need therefore double assistance. Our minds must be enlightened; our hearts constrained."[2] True enough! We too must start with this confession, if we would learn God's ways.

Advancing in God's School

One of the things a superior student should care about once he or she is admitted to a good school is achieving a well-rounded education. There is not much concern about that in many schools today because the quality of education has declined. Much of today's education is essentially only learning a trade so a person can earn a decent living. This is fine as far as it goes, but God's people need to be well-rounded, developing their intellects as well as their skills. A well-rounded student will develop in many areas of knowledge, such as the humanities, social sciences, physical sciences, art, music, and perhaps drama. A well-rounded person will not forget physical development either, but will keep his or her body in shape.

It is useful to think in terms of a balanced education to understand what is going on next in Psalm 119. A well-rounded education is education for the whole person, and this is what the psalmist wants for himself. What is the best way to achieve a well-rounded education in God's school? Verses 34–37 teach that it is by keeping God's Word before one's mind, feet, heart, and eyes—four important parts of the body that must be under God's control.

The Mind

"Give me understanding" (v. 34). The wisdom the writer seeks is practical. He doesn't want merely to know God's law but to walk according to it. It *is* necessary to know God's law. In fact it is necessary to have an intellectual understanding of God's ways before we can apply his Word. We cannot apply what we don't know. That is why Paul began the application section of Romans with words about the renewal of the mind (Rom. 12:1–2). The psalmist also begins with the mind, asking God to help him understand the Bible.

Does your mind matter? Years ago John R. W. Stott, Rector Emeritus of All Souls Church in London, wrote a little book insisting that it does. It is titled, significantly enough, *Your Mind Matters*.[3] It deals with six areas of Christian living, and Stott argues that each is impossible without a proper and energetic use of our minds. These six areas are Christian worship, Christian faith, Christian holiness, Christian guidance, Christian evangelism, and Christian ministry.

Our minds matter in *worship* because worship is honoring God for who he is, and to do that we need to understand something about God's attributes. We must praise him for being sovereign, holy, merciful, wise, omniscient—all that he is. Without a true understanding of God's attributes, worship becomes only an emotional binge in which we indulge our feelings.

Our minds matter for *faith* because faith is believing and acting on the word or promises of God, and to believe God's promises we must understand what they are. Apart from a right use of the mind, faith becomes only a feeling or, worse yet, wishful thinking.

Our minds matter for growth in *holiness,* which is what we are chiefly concerned about in this psalm, because growth in holiness (sanctification) is not a matter of emotions or simply following a formula for living—the two most popular approaches to sanctification today. Growth in holiness is knowing what God has done in us when he joined us to Christ and then acting on it because there is really nothing else we can do. It is knowing that we cannot go back to being what we were; therefore there is no other direction for us to go but forward.[4]

Our minds matter in seeking personal *guidance* as to how we should live and what decisions we must make because the principles by which we must be guided are in the Bible. God does not guide us by mystical revelations, and we cannot count on God's providential ordering of events alone, though he does indeed order all things. The chief and usually the only way God guides is by the Bible. To be guided by God we need to study to understand God's Word and then apply its principles. That cannot be done without thinking.

Our minds matter in *evangelism* because if a person must have faith to be saved and if faith is responding to the Word of God and acting on it, then we must present the teaching of the Bible and the claims of Jesus Christ so others can understand them. They must know what they are "believing." If they do not understand what they are believing and therefore are only able to respond emotionally, their "faith" is not a true faith and theirs is not a true conversion.

Finally, our minds matter in *ministry,* first, in seeking out a sphere of service (What am I good at? Where do my spiritual gifts lie? What is God leading me to do for him?) and, second, to serve well in that sphere (How should I go about the work I have been given?).

Stott argues that anti-intellectualism is "part of the fashion of the world and therefore a form of worldliness." He asks pointedly, "Has God created us rational beings, and shall we deny our humanity which he has given us? Has God spoken to us, and shall we not listen to his words? Has God renewed our mind through Christ, and shall we not think with it?"[5]

The Feet

"Direct me in the path of your commands" (v. 35). The third verse in this section teaches that if we are going to make progress in God's school, we also need God's Word before our feet, to guide our paths. Puritan commentator Thomas Manton wrote on Psalm 119:

> David, in the former verses, had begged for light, now for strength to walk according to this light. We need not only light to know our way, but a heart to walk in it. Direction is necessary because of the blindness of our minds; and the effectual impulsions of grace are necessary because of the weakness of our hearts.[6]

What is this way in which we should walk? The Hebrew word translated "path" is from a root verb meaning "to tread" and therefore means "the trodden way" or an accustomed trail, not a new direction. In other words, it is a well-worn path because of the many who have walked it before us. Herbert Lockyer speaks of "an accustomed trail, plain with the track of all the pious pilgrims' feet of past times."[7]

This reminds me of Jeremiah 6:16, a verse that meant so much to the Puritans and others who have come after them. They understood it as direction for what they should be doing.

> Stand at the crossroads and look;
>   ask for the ancient paths,
> ask where the good way is, and walk in it.

We live in an age of constant innovations. Everything old is thought to be bad, and what is new is good. Even old products are sold by giving them a new twist or look: the new Ford Taurus or new improved Efferdent. We tend to think this way too, because of our cultural environment. The psalm reminds us that the Lord's way is not a new or novel way, but rather that old established way in which the people of God have walked from the very beginning of God's dealings with our race.

In terms of the Christian life we are not innovators; we are imitators. We want to be like those who have gone before us and walk as they walked. We want to be like Abraham and Moses and David and the apostle Paul and the Reformers and the Puritans and the spiritual giants of our own time. But we also remember that this is a narrow path and there are only a few who walk in it (Matt. 7:13–14). The reason for this has to do with our heart, as seen in the next section.

The Heart

"Turn my heart toward your statutes" (v. 36). To make progress in God's school we not only have to understand what the way of God is and have strength to walk in it, directing our feet along the old, established path, we must also *want* to walk in it. This is what the poet prays for next when he implores, "Turn my heart toward your statutes and not toward selfish gain."

This is the first time in this stanza that the writer has mentioned a negative alternative to what he is asking God to help him do. He is asking God to turn his heart toward the Bible *rather than* allowing him to pursue selfish gain. This means that, for the first time, he is confessing to a potentially divided mind. He wants to pursue God's law, but he knows his heart and is aware that he could very well also decline into covetousness, which is the ruin of the soul. Jesus said, "You cannot serve both God and Money" (Matt. 6:24). The psalmist knew that. Moreover, he knew the appeal riches have and his inclination to pursue them. So he asks God to incline his heart away from riches and toward God and his law.

The Eyes

"Turn my eyes away from worthless things" (v. 37). The fourth part of the body that we need to have under control to pursue God and his commandments is the eyes. Eyes are needed to study God's Word. But the psalmist does not even speak of what the eyes should be turned toward, only what he wants them to be turned from. He wants to be delivered from "worthless things" or vanities.

This verse follows naturally from the one before it, for once the writer has begun to consider what might keep him from a profitable study of the Bible, he realizes that he is tempted by more than mere riches. There are many worthless things and they are all alluring. If we are to advance in God's school, we must fix our eyes on the things of God, which are lasting, rather than the things of this world, which are passing away.

Verse 37 occurs in *Pilgrim's Progress* at a well-known point in the narrative. It is when Christian and Faithful come to Vanity Fair on their way to the Celestial City. Here all the merchandise of the world is for sale, but those who are on their way to the Celestial City do not fit in with these people and when they are asked to stop and buy, they put their hands to their ears and run away crying, "Turn away mine eyes from beholding Vanity," and look toward heaven to show that the business of their lives is in that place.[8] That sentence—"Turn away mine eyes from beholding Vanity"—is Psalm 119:37. It is the Christian's only wise response to the vanities of this world.[9]

Encouragement in God's School

Faced by temptations and the dangers of life, the psalmist is aware that he needs help. But where is help to be found?

The only help is from God, and the only reason he can hope for God's help is that God has promised to help him. That is the point of verse 38: "Fulfill your promise to your servant, so that you may be feared."

What promise is that? There is no reason to think he is singling out any one promise. Rather he is thinking of the entire Word of God, as he has been doing all along. The noun translated "promise" here is actually one of the Hebrew terms for "word" (*'imrah*), sometimes translated "a saying" since it comes from the verb "to say." The King James Bible and the Revised Version translate it as "word" throughout. The Jerusalem and New English Bibles use "promise." The Revised Standard Version has a combination of the two. The reason for the choice of *'imrah* is that the psalmist knows that if he is to complete his course of study he will have to live by God's Word constantly and in all its parts, not picking and choosing what he wants to obey. This verse is a perfect Old Testament expression of what Jesus said to Satan when he was tempted by him to turn stones into bread. He told him, "Man does not live on bread alone, but on every word that comes from the mouth of God" (Matt. 4:4, quoting Deut. 8:3). True life comes by way of God's Word.

Why, then, does the verse speak of God fulfilling his word of promise to the psalmist? It is because, in a sense, all of God's Word is a promise—a promise of life to those who repent of sin and determine to go in God's way and a promise of death and judgment for those who reject the gospel message. The psalmist is clinging to the promise of life because he fears, or stands in awe of, God. If we are to profit from his example, we must do the same. We must live by every word from his mouth.

On Not Dropping Out of God's School

The last two verses of this section of the psalm bring in a new idea that can be related to the mistake of dropping out of an academic program. Dropouts are a major problem today, particularly at the high school level. When young people drop out of high school, as many do, especially from city schools, there is very little future for them. They will have to labor at unskilled, low-paying jobs. Some will get involved in crime and may make money by selling drugs. It was because of the acute nature of this problem in Philadelphia that Tenth Presbyterian Church began City Center Academy, our high school.

The psalmist says that "disgrace" ("reproach," as some of the versions have it) might cause him to drop out. "Take away the disgrace I dread, for your laws are good," he implores.

Disgrace in verse 39 can be thought of in either of two ways. On the one hand, it could be the disgrace brought on by God because of the writer's sin. That is, he could disgrace himself by his disobedience. On the other hand, it could be disgrace heaped on him by sinners because of his faithful adherence to God's law.

Franz Delitzsch argues that "the reproach which the poet fears in verse 39 is not the reproach of confessing, but of denying God."[10] Alexander Maclaren interprets the verse as describing reproach before God too, because it gives a better meaning to the words "for your laws are good."[11] However, H. C. Leupold chooses the second interpretation—that it is referring to reproach heaped on the psalmist by sinful men—for exactly the same reason, that it gives a better sense to the second half of verse 39: "God's ordinances should be confessed and upheld, and whatever reproach we may suffer in upholding them God is readily able to turn away from us."[12] Thomas Manton thinks it is the reproach of enemies too: "the reproach which was like to be his lot and portion in the world, through the malice of his enemies."[13]

This disagreement probably cannot be resolved with certainty, at least at this stage of our scholarship. But, in either case, the danger is the same: the danger of dropping out of

God's school due either to personal failure or because of other people's scorn. When we are tempted to drop out, we must remember Jesus' words: "All men will hate you because of me, but he who stands firm to the end will be saved" (Matt. 10:22). It means that Christians always eventually persevere. And so must you if you are a genuine Christian.

5
Finding God in His Word

May your unfailing love come to me, O LORD,
  your salvation according to your promise;
then I will answer the one who taunts me,
  for I trust in your word.
Do not snatch the word of truth from my mouth,
  for I have put my hope in your laws.
I will always obey your law,
  for ever and ever.
I walk about in freedom,
  for I have sought out your precepts.
I will speak of your statutes before kings
  and will not be put to shame,
for I delight in your commands
  because I love them.
I lift up my hands to your commands, which I love,
  and I meditate on your decrees.

Remember your word to your servant,
  for you have given me hope.
My comfort in my suffering is this:
  Your promise preserves my life.
The arrogant mock me without restraint,
  but I do not turn from your law.

I remember your ancient laws, O LORD,
    and I find comfort in them.
Indignation grips me because of the wicked,
    who have forsaken your law.
Your decrees are the theme of my song
    wherever I lodge.
In the night I remember your name, O LORD,
    and I will keep your law.
This has been my practice:
    I obey your precepts.

You are my portion, O LORD;
    I have promised to obey your words.
I have sought your face with all my heart;
    be gracious to me according to your promise.
I have considered my ways
    and have turned my steps to your statutes.
I will hasten and not delay
    to obey your commands.
Though the wicked bind me with ropes,
    I will not forget your law.
At midnight I rise to give you thanks
    for your righteous laws.
I am a friend to all who fear you,
    to all who follow your precepts.
The earth is filled with your love, O LORD;
    teach me your decrees.

Psalm 119:41–64

BRUCE WALTKE IS A PROFESSOR OF OLD TESTAMENT STUDIES AT Reformed Theological Seminary in Orlando, Florida, and a former teacher at a number of evangelical schools, including Dallas Seminary, Westminster Theological Seminary in Philadelphia, and Regent College, Vancouver, British Columbia. He is an outstanding scholar and he has written an excellent book in which he testifies to the importance of prayer in getting to know God through Bible study.

He explains that early in his life he used to read the Bible for its academic merit, getting nothing out of it. But one day he heard a preacher say that it is necessary to ask God for enlightenment. So he began praying, "Lord, speak to me through your Word." At first his reading seemed much the same. "But soon," he writes, "within three weeks of praying that prayer as I read, my heart began to burn within me. I started to see new things in Scripture. God began revealing to me how his Word should change my life. I developed a love for his teaching. God heard my prayer and began to speak to me through his Word."[1]

What Waltke found is what the writer of Psalm 119 tells us, particularly in the next three sections of his psalm, namely that the purpose of Bible study is not merely to get to know the Bible in some abstract or academic sense. The purpose of Bible study should be to get to know God. The key to this goal is prayerful Bible study.

The psalmist has been speaking this way all along, of course. He has used the first person pronoun more than is the case in other psalms and he has addressed God directly again and again. It is always "I" and "you." But in these three stanzas *(waw, zayin,* and *heth)* the psalmist rises to new heights in expressing his desire to know the God of love and all comfort. The climax comes in verse 57, when he declares, "You are my portion, O LORD."

Finding God's Love

The first of these three stanzas concentrates on God's love, which is the most wonderful of his attributes and certainly a fitting place for the psalmist to begin. Surprisingly, it is the first stanza in the psalm in which he speaks of God's love. And not only that, it is also the first stanza in which he speaks of God's salvation. The two words occur together in verse 41: May your unfailing love come to me, O LORD, your salvation according to your promise.

It may seem surprising that this is the first time the writer has mentioned God's love, but it is not the least bit surprising that the first time he mentions love, he also mentions salvation. This is because the proof of God's love is seen in his provision of salvation for sinners. It is out of the great love of God that this salvation comes.

When the Old Testament saints wrote about salvation they could only have had a rudimentary idea about all that was involved. But we live on the far side of the cross and know how the love of God and the death of Christ came together. We remember how the apostle Paul linked the two ideas in Romans 5: "Very rarely will anyone die for a righteous man, though for a good man someone might possibly dare to die. But God demonstrates his own love for us in this: While we were still sinners, Christ died for us" (vv. 7–8). Nor can we forget John 3:16, the best known verse in the Bible: "For God so loved the world that he gave his one and only Son, that whoever believes in him shall not perish but have eternal life."

We have already discovered that the author of this psalm is a practical man in the matter of his religion. So at this point he does not dwell at length on God's love itself but instead mentions two important results of getting to know God's love personally.

1. *Obedience.* "I will always obey your law, for ever and ever" (v. 44). Does it seem surprising that one of the first results of coming to know God as a God of love is obedience? It does to many people, but the reason it does is that they have an inadequate and even warped idea of what love means. We think of love as mere sentimentality, a feeling to be enjoyed and wallowed in. But in the Bible, love is a relationship issuing in moral actions. Jesus taught this to his disci-

ples. He told them, "If you love me, you will obey what I command" (John 14:15).

It is worth noting that the words translated "always," "for ever" and "ever" render three different Hebrew words that come at the very end of the verse, like this: always, eternally, and for ever. It is an effective way of saying that the psalmist's obedience is going to go on and on. There will never be a time when the godly stop obeying God.

2. *Speaking about God's love to others.* The second result of getting to know about God's love is a compulsion to speak about God and his love to others. This point is emphasized strongly in this stanza, particularly the writer's desire to speak about God to those who are opposed to him and who ridicule righteous persons like himself. "Then I will answer the one who taunts me," says the psalmist (v. 42). "Do not snatch the word of truth from my mouth," he adds (v. 43). And still again, "I will speak of your statutes before kings and will not be put to shame" (v. 46).

Historians have often referred to this last verse to describe Martin Luther's heroic stand before the Diet of Worms. Luther had been summoned to Worms to appear before the newly elected emperor Charles V and the assembled champions of the church to answer for heresies that were believed to be in his writings. It was an ominous moment because others, who had been similarly summoned, had been arrested and then cruelly executed for their supposed offenses against both church and state. Everyone remembered John Huss, who had been burned at Constance on the Rhine about a hundred years before. Like Huss, Luther could have been martyred.

Luther stood before the council on April 18, 1521, after a night of prayer and serious self-examination. The moderator of the assembly pointed to a table holding Luther's books. "Will you retract these writings?" he asked.

Earlier Luther had attempted to draw the council into a discussion of the teachings themselves, but nobody wanted to debate with Luther. Instead he was told to give a yes or no answer. "Will you, or will you not retract?" The demand was insistent.

Luther replied:

> Since your most serene majesty and your high mightiness require from me a clear, simple, and precise answer, I will give you one, and it is this: I cannot submit my faith either to the pope or to the councils, because it is clear to me as the day that they have frequently erred and contradicted each other. Unless therefore I am convinced by the testimony of Scripture, or by the clearest reasoning—unless I am persuaded by means of the passages I have quoted—and unless they thus render my conscience bound by the Word of God, I cannot and I will not retract, for it is unsafe for a Christian to speak against his conscience. Here I stand. I can do no other. May God help me. Amen.[2]

In this way Martin Luther did exactly what Psalm 119:46 is describing. He spoke of God's statutes before kings and he was not put to shame.[3]

We can summarize this stanza of the psalm by noting that it deals with three kinds of love: (1) God's love for us disclosed in his provision of salvation, which the writer speaks of finding; (2) our love for God, which is implied in the matter of obedience; and (3) love of God's commandments, which results in our wanting to tell others about them (vv. 47–48). A measure of your love for God is your willingness to tell others about God's commands and God's love. If you love God and thus also love the Word, how can you not tell others about him?[4]

Finding God's Comfort

The theme of getting to know God by means of a prayerful study of the Scriptures continues in stanza seven, the *zayin* stanza. The emphasis here is on finding God to be a comfort in life's sufferings. Comfort is mentioned twice, in verses 50 and 52.

My comfort in my suffering is this:
  Your promise preserves my life.

I remember your ancient laws, O LORD,
  and I find comfort in them.

It is an interesting thing about this stanza, dealing as it does with suffering, that there is only one direct prayer to God for help: "Remember your word to your servant, for you have given me hope" (v. 49). Even this verse does not specifically ask to be delivered from suffering.

All the other verses of the stanza are the writer's statements that he trusts what God has written in his law and will continue to love it and obey its teachings. It is a way of acknowledging that suffering is common to human beings. We are not always able to avoid it. The important thing is not escaping the suffering, even with God's help, but continuing to trust God and prove him a genuine source of comfort even while we are going through the trial.

One prominent word in this stanza is *remember*. It occurs three times in verses 49, 52, and 55. In the first case, it is an appeal to God to remember his words of promise, which the writer is sure he will do. This is his source of comfort. In the next two uses of the word *remember*, the psalmist asserts that *he* will remember. He will remember God's "ancient laws" (v. 52) and God's "name" (v. 55). In other words, he will use his times of suffering to meditate on God's Word and character, knowing that one purpose of his suffering must be to give him time to get to know God better.

And he won't just meditate! He will sing! Verse 54 speaks of singing in the midst of suffering, so wonderful is God's comfort in such times. Is that really possible? Of course. Paul and Silas sang in prison at Philippi, after having been severely beaten. And they were doing it in the middle of the night, which is another thing the psalmist mentions ("In the night

I remember your name, O LORD"). The story in Acts says, "About midnight Paul and Silas were praying and singing hymns to God, and the other prisoners were listening to them" (Acts 16:25). After witnessing a faith like that, it is no wonder that the Philippian jailer and many others believed on the Jesus whom Paul and Silas proclaimed and that God established a strong enduring church in that city. It was this church that backed Paul's missionary work, sending him money time and again to help with his expenses (Phil. 4:15–16).

It has always been natural for Christians to sing of what is lodged joyfully in their hearts, and their worship services have always been characterized by great hymn singing. People in the world do not sing very much today, though they listen to other people perform songs for them. Many of these songs are not joyful but ugly. They are ugly because life for our contemporaries is ugly. How beautiful are the hymns of Christians in such ugly times as ours!

Henry Wadsworth Longfellow, the American poet who gave us "Evangeline" and "The Song of Hiawatha," wrote this about musical renderings of God's Word:

> Such songs have power to quiet
> The restless pulse of care,
> And come like the benediction
> That follows after prayer.
> And the night shall be filled with music,
> And the cares that infest the day
> Shall fold their tents like the Arabs,
> And as silently steal away.

The singing of Christians does not make the causes of their sorrows go away—though the Lord sometimes does that himself—but it does lift their spirits and testifies to the goodness of God who provides comfort even in bad times.

Finding God Himself

Everything we have looked at so far leads to stanza eight (the *heth* stanza, the last of this little grouping of three), and to its key verse: "You are my portion, O LORD" (v. 57). The purpose of a prayerful study of God's Word is not just to find comfort or even just to get to know one aspect of God's character—even one as important as love—but the purpose of a prayerful study of God's Word is to get to know and to possess God himself. Charles Haddon Spurgeon, the nineteenth-century Baptist evangelist and preacher, wrote wisely of this stanza, "In this section the psalmist seems to take firm hold upon God himself: appropriating him (v. 57), crying out for him (v. 58), returning to him (v. 59), solacing himself in him (vv. 61–62), associating with his people (v. 63), and sighing for personal experience of his goodness (v. 64)."[5]

When the psalmist wrote that God was his "portion" he was using a word that had great meaning in Jewish religious history. When the Israelite tribes came out of the desert and made their conquest of the land of Canaan and every tribe received its appointed portion, the priestly tribe of Levi did not receive land. Instead, they were given forty-eight priestly cities scattered throughout the land and were to live there so that their priestly service would always be widely available. They had no land but they were given something better. It was said of them that they had no portion (inheritance) in the land because their portion (inheritance) was the Lord (see Josh. 13:33).[6]

This is what lies behind the key verse of this stanza. The writer is saying that, like the Levites, he wants his portion of divine blessing to be God himself, since nothing is better and nothing will ever fully satisfy his or anyone else's heart but God himself. To possess God is truly to have everything.

It requires effort to acquire this treasure, however. This is because God is discovered in his Word—this is the single most important teaching of Psalm 119—and it requires effort to get to know the Bible. It is not easily mastered. Therefore, in the remaining verses of this stanza the psalmist encourages us in our study of the Bible by telling what he has done to possess God.

He sought God's face (v. 58). To seek God's face means to seek God himself, to labor at getting to know him on a personal basis. Will those who seek God earnestly find him? Of course! The promise that if we seek God we will find him is a major theme of Scripture.

David testified, "If you seek him, he will be found by you" (1 Chron. 28:9; see also 2 Chron. 15:2). God told the exiles in Babylon through Jeremiah, "You will seek me and find me when you seek me with all your heart. I will be found by you" (Jer. 29:13–14). And Jesus said, speaking of prayer, "Ask and it will be given to you; seek and you will find; knock and the door will be opened to you" (Matt. 7:7). If that applies to such common things as food and clothing and a place to live, as it does, can we suppose that it will apply any less to the pursuit of God himself? Those who seek God will surely find him.

He followed God's statutes (v. 59). If we follow God's statutes, we follow after or live by God's Word as a way of life. Blaise Pascal, brilliant French philosopher and devout Christian, loved Psalm 119. He is another person who memorized it and he called verse 59 "the turning point of man's character and destiny."[7] He meant that it is vital for every person to consider his or her ways, understand that our ways are destructive and will lead us to destruction, and then make an about-face and determine to go in God's way instead.

He obeyed God's commands (v. 60). To find God is to find the one who is the King of the universe and our Lord. Therefore it is necessary and inevitable that we obey him. Jesus asked pointedly, "Why do you call me 'Lord, Lord,' and do not do what I say?" (Luke 6:46). He meant that those who are his true disciples will obey him and that those who do not obey him are not disciples. This does not mean that Christians are sinless. We obviously are not. But it does mean that if we do not work at obeying God's commands, we are not Christians.

He remembered God's law (v. 61). One of the great problems with trying to live as a Christian is that we forget God's Word, indeed even his many mercies to us. The psalmist determined not to forget. He wanted to remember God's law whatever the circumstances, so he might be encouraged by it and follow it.

He thanked God for his laws (v. 62). The writer of this psalm is no grim pedant, merely plodding after God's law with a dour determination to conform to it. He recognized that God's law is good, the greatest of all treasures. Therefore he thanked God for it. Indeed, he made God's decrees the theme of his midnight melodies (vv. 54–55).

He identified with others who also follow God's precepts (v. 63). This is the last point, and it is an important one. The psalmist recognized that he was not alone in his chosen way of life. There were others moving along the same devout path, other believers traveling along with him. He wanted to be their friend, to encourage them, and to be encouraged by them. H. C. Leupold wrote that the last words of this stanza put the writer into "that select company of men who both fear the Lord and keep his precepts," adding that "in the last analysis this is the procedure followed by all true children of God."[8]

It is a great blessing to belong to the company of such saints. It is something any true Christian will desire.

6

Affliction

Do good to your servant
    according to your word, O LORD.
Teach me knowledge and good judgment,
    for I believe in your commands.
Before I was afflicted I went astray,
    but now I obey your word.
You are good, and what you do is good;
    teach me your decrees.
Though the arrogant have smeared me with lies,
    I keep your precepts with all my heart.
Their hearts are callous and unfeeling,
    but I delight in your law.
It was good for me to be afflicted
    so that I might learn your decrees.
The law from your mouth is more precious to me
    than thousands of pieces of silver and gold.

Your hands made me and formed me;
    give me understanding to learn your commands.
May those who fear you rejoice when they see me,
    for I have put my hope in your word.
I know, O LORD, that your laws are righteous,

and in faithfulness you have afflicted me.
May your unfailing love be my comfort,
    according to your promise to your servant.
Let your compassion come to me that I may live,
    for your law is my delight.
May the arrogant be put to shame for wronging me
        without cause;
    but I will meditate on your precepts.
May those who fear you turn to me,
    those who understand your statutes.
May my heart be blameless toward your decrees,
    that I may not be put to shame.

My soul faints with longing for your salvation,
    but I have put my hope in your word.
My eyes fail, looking for your promise;
    I say, "When will you comfort me?"
Though I am like a wineskin in the smoke,
    I do not forget your decrees.
How long must your servant wait?
    When will you punish my persecutors?
The arrogant dig pitfalls for me,
    contrary to your law.
All your commands are trustworthy;
    help me, for men persecute me without cause.
They almost wiped me from the earth,
    but I have not forsaken your precepts.
Preserve my life according to your love,
    and I will obey the statutes of your mouth.

                                        Psalm 119:65–88

MOST PEOPLE HAVE HEARD THE TIRED ATHEISTIC REBUTTAL
to Christianity based on the presence of suffering in the world.

It has been expressed in different ways depending on the viewpoint of the unbeliever who utters it. But one common form of the rebuttal goes like this: If God were good, he would wish to make his creatures happy; and if God were almighty, he would be able to do what he wished. But his creatures are not happy. Therefore God lacks either goodness or power or both.[1] That objection is insulting in its superficiality, for it assumes that the ultimate good in this world is our lack of suffering and that the only possible factors in our quandary are the alleged benevolence and alleged omnipotence of God.

Any serious thinker and all Christians know that there is more to the problem of suffering than this. Nevertheless, the problem of pain is a big one. I remember a seminary course on suffering that called pain the "one great unsolved problem of Christian theology." I do not think it is an utterly unsolved problem. But pain is nevertheless a real and inescapable problem since everyone goes through some suffering at some time.

The psalmist endured a lot of it. We have already looked at some of this man's trials in an earlier chapter, focusing on those trials that came because of his determination to live faithfully by God's Word. In these three stanzas of the psalm *(teth, yodh,* and *kaph)*, we see trials of a much broader nature, trials that the writer refers to as afflictions. That is the new word in these stanzas: "afflicted." It occurs three times in verses 65–88, twice in stanza nine (vv. 67, 71), once in stanza ten (verse 75), and, although it does not actually occur in stanza eleven, that stanza describes the poet's afflictions in the saddest and most pitiful language of all.

Taking these stanzas together and in sequence, they teach us important things about the purpose, source, and end result of suffering in the life of the Christian.

"What You Do Is Good"

Even though we're dealing here with suffering and God's purposes in it, I need to say at the start that affliction is not the most frequently mentioned matter in stanza nine. The most prominent word in these verses is *good*. There is a reason for this. This is the *teth* stanza. *Teth* is the first letter of the Hebrew word "good" *(tov),* so it was a natural thought for the composer of the psalm to use *good* at the beginning of these verses. The word occurs at the beginning of five of the eight verses in this stanza, in verses 65, 66, 68, 71, and 72.

Of course, it is not just because the word for "good" begins with the letter *teth* that the psalmist reflects on what is good so often. It is because this is what he has discovered about affliction. He has discovered that suffering is good when it flows from God's unvarying goodness toward us. Affliction is not good in itself and it does not usually seem good to us when we are enduring it, but it has a good purpose when God sends it, as he frequently does to his greatly cherished children.

Here are the verses that begin with the word "good."

Verse 65: "Do good to your servant according to your word, O Lord." This is a general statement, asking God to do good to the psalmist, which God has done and is certain to continue doing. Some writers call this the text for which the rest of the stanza is the sermon. One way God does good is by sending afflictions.

Verse 66: "Teach me knowledge and good judgment, for I believe in your commands." This is an elaboration of the general statement, explaining that the good the psalmist wants is not merely through the affliction itself, but rather through knowledge of God's ways leading to good judgment, which he was able to learn because of his suffering. Every believer needs such knowledge and the good judgment that is related to it.

Verse 68: "You are good, and what you do is good; teach me your decrees." This is the middle verse of the five, and it is most important, pivotal. It anchors goodness to the very nature of God; God is good and he is always doing good.

Verse 71: "It was good for me to be afflicted so that I might learn your decrees." This verse applies the general goodness of God's character to the specific matter of the psalmist's affliction. Since God is good and since he sends suffering, the suffering itself must have a good purpose. This verse is an exact equivalent of Romans 8:28, which we probably know better: "And we know that in all things God works for the good of those who love him, who have been called according to his purpose."

Verse 72: "The law from your mouth is more precious [good] to me than thousands of pieces of silver and gold." This verse returns to the theme of God's Word, which the writer says is better even than many thousands of pieces of gold and silver.

Herbert Lockyer recounts a story concerning the largest Bible in the world. It is a Hebrew manuscript weighing 320 pounds and is in the Vatican library. Long ago a group of Italian Jews asked to see this Bible and when they had seen it, they told their friends in Venice about the manuscript's existence. The result was that a syndicate of Russian Jews tried to buy it, offering the church the weight of the book in gold. Julius the Second was Pope at that time and he refused the offer, even though the value of such a large amount of gold was enormous. Wrote Lockyer, "Thousands of gold and silver pieces are nothing in comparison with the inestimably precious Word of God."[2] Today we can possess multiple copies of God's Word for a very small amount of money. But do we value it? In many cases, I am afraid we do not.

Purpose of Affliction

Why do the righteous suffer? What is the purpose of affliction in their lives? When we look for the answers that are given in the Bible as a whole, we find that there are various explanations, which is not surprising since this is not a simple problem.

First, some suffering is simply *the common lot of man*. We live in an imperfect world. We get hurt; we get sick; we die. It is not always correct to read great meaning into such afflictions. Jesus seemed to take that view of the fall of the tower of Siloam that killed eighteen people and to the killing of some Galileans by Pilate's soldiers. He denied that these individuals were more deserving of death than others, noting instead, "Unless you repent, you too will all perish" (Luke 13:5). Job said, "Man is born to trouble as surely as sparks fly upward" (Job 5:7).

Second, there is suffering that is *corrective*. This is the most obvious category of suffering for most Christians, and it is what the poet is chiefly speaking of in this psalm when he says, "Before I was afflicted I went astray, but now I obey your word" (v. 67). He is admitting that the afflictions he endured were sent by God to get him back onto the path of obeying God's Word.

Third, some suffering is *constructive*. That is, it is used by God to sharpen our skills and develop our character, just like physical exercise develops stronger muscles and endurance. A common saying around exercise facilities is: "No pain, no gain." Paul wrote of this purpose for suffering in Romans 5: "Suffering produces perseverance; perseverance, character; and character, hope" (vv. 3–4).

Fourth, some suffering is *Christ-glorifying*. The afflictions of the man born blind were of this nature, for Jesus explained that he had been suffering neither for his own sin nor for that of his parents, but only "that the work of God might be displayed in his life" (John 9:3). Hard as this may be for many people to accept, Jesus meant that the blind man had been called to endure blindness his whole life so that, at this point in history, Jesus might heal him and bring glory to God as the one who gives physical and spiritual sight.

The fifth purpose of suffering is *cosmic,* and Job is the Bible's most profound and detailed exploration of this purpose. The suffering of Job and others like him demonstrates before Satan and the angels that a person can love and trust God for who God is in himself and not merely for what the person can get from God.[3]

Psalm 119:65–88 is exploring the second of these five uses of affliction in the believer's life (corrective), because this is what the writer says God did with him. God sent affliction into his life as a divine corrective to direct him into right paths so that he would know and obey God's Word. The writer explores the purpose of affliction in stanza nine and gives two reasons it was good for him.

1. *Obedience* (v. 67). The first thing the writer says God did by sending suffering into his life was to teach him obedience: "Before I was afflicted I went astray, but now I obey your word."

The Hebrew of this verse does not suggest that the writer had deliberately and willfully plunged into sin and was then reproved by God and returned to the path of righteousness. Going astray here has to do mostly with the writer's ignorance. It means that before God brought affliction into his life, he trusted his own judgment and wandered into vain and harmful paths. When things did not go well for him, he turned to God's Word, discovered the right way to live, and began to obey the Bible's teachings.

We can be encouraged in our suffering by remembering that the Bible says even of Jesus, "Although he was a son, he learned obedience from what he suffered" (Heb. 5:8).

2. *Greater understanding of God's ways* (v. 71). The second blessing the psalmist says he got from suffering was greater understanding of God's decrees in Scripture. "It was good for me to be afflicted so that I might learn your decrees."

We might think that the order of these two verses is reversed, since knowing God's decrees should precede obeying them. That is true, but it is not what the psalmist means here. When he read God's law, he knew it well enough to obey it then, and did. But as he was continually driven to the study of the Word by continuing afflictions, he came to understand the Bible more fully and at deeper and deeper levels.

This is what Martin Luther meant when he confessed, "I never knew the meaning of God's word, until I came into affliction. I have always found it one of my best schoolmasters."[4] Luther already understood God's Word; he had been teaching it. But he came to understand it more deeply when God led him through affliction.

Source of Affliction

The tenth stanza of Psalm 119 is the *yodh* stanza, the Hebrew letter Jesus referred to when he said, "Until heaven and earth disappear, not the smallest letter, not the least stroke of a pen, will by any means disappear from the Law until everything is accomplished" (Matt. 5:18). The *yodh* is a mere dash of a letter, but in Psalm 119 the *yodh* section does not deal with trifles. On the contrary, like the stanza before it and the stanza following, it deals with the afflictions that come into the life of the trusting child of God.

What does this second stanza add to the study of affliction? It adds explicitly what was only assumed earlier, namely, that God is the ultimate source of the affliction. "I know, O LORD, that your laws are righteous, and in faithfulness you have afflicted me" (v. 75).

This is an important insight for any believer to possess, and that is why the stanza begins as it does. It is about the source of affliction. It begins not by mentioning the psalmist's suffering, however, but by confessing that he was "made" and "formed" by God (v. 73). What is the point of that? The reference to God's forming him is a deliberate echo of Genesis 2, where God is said to have "formed the man from the dust of the ground and breathed into his nostrils the breath of life" (Gen. 2:7). The point of the reference is that God did not make man as the beasts, which have no understanding. Man was made to know and understand the ways of God. The psalmist, in the second half of verse 73, prays for the gift of understanding God's commands.

So now we ask: What does he come to understand? Quite a few things, it would seem, and all of them important.

God is faithful even in the affliction (v. 75). Faithful to what or to whom? If the affliction were occasioned by the poet's sin, the word *faithful* might refer to God's faithfulness to his own righteousness and justice. The judge of all the earth must punish sin. Yet we have had no reason to think that the writer's afflictions were caused by his sin, so the faithfulness mentioned here probably refers to God's faithfulness to the psalmist, a proof that he continues to love him and is helping him grow and mature through affliction. We need to see that ourselves when things are not going exactly as we would wish.

God's unfailing love is a comfort (v. 76). God sent afflictions to the psalmist because of God's unfailing love. The fact that suffering's source and reason is God's love comforts the psalmist even while he is going through his trials. And he does need comfort. He had asked God for understanding concerning his afflictions, and these stanzas show that God gave it to him. Even so, suffering is bitter and the afflicted one needs comfort.

God is compassionate (v. 77). The word signifies "mercy," and mercy by definition is grace shown to those who are undeserving, those who, in fact, merit the exact opposite. But God *is* merciful. His very name is mercy (see Exod. 34:6–7). Thus, regardless of what we are going through and whether it is the result of our sin or not and whether we have brought it on ourselves or not, we can appeal to God's mercy and be assured that we will find it.

One's handling of suffering can be an encouragement to other believers (v. 79, also v. 74). For the most part the poet has been thinking about and praying for himself, but he realizes here that what happens to him and how he reacts to it can be either a source of discouragement or a source of encouragement to others. He wants to be an encouragement. Hence, his two prayers: "May those who fear you rejoice when they see me" (v. 74) and "May those who fear you turn to me, those who understand your statutes" (v. 79). He desires to handle his affliction in such a way that other believers will be encouraged when they see him.

In the latter half of this stanza the writer voices three prayers. He prays for the arrogant, that they might be put to shame (v. 78). He prays for other believers, that they might be encouraged by his example (v. 79). And he prays for himself, that he might be able to live blamelessly according to God's decrees (v. 80). The heathen used to wish for "a sound mind in a sound body." The psalmist wants more. He wants "a sound heart," blameless because it is grounded in the Word of God.

Result of Affliction

The last of these three stanzas brings us to the lowest point in the psalm, placed here just before the halfway mark. Spurgeon wrote, "This octave is the midnight of the psalm, and very dark and black it is." But he also noted that even in the blackness, "stars . . . shine out, and the last verse gives promise of the dawn."[5] It may be significant in this respect that verse 84 is the first in the psalm to fail to mention the Word of God or any of the ten or so synonyms for it. Was it the case, when the psalmist was most down, that he temporarily lost sight of God's Word?

This stanza has a great deal to say about the psalmist's enemies, as though at this point his thoughts were focused on them. He has spoken of them before and will again, though they assume a far less threatening role from stanza twelve to the end. Here he reports that these enemies have been persecuting him (v. 84), digging pitfalls for him (v. 85), and trying to wipe him from the earth (v. 87). The last phrase is literally "in the earth," which seems pointless until we remember verse 85, which says that his enemies were digging pits for him. That is how they wanted to get him "in the earth." They wanted to kill and bury him. No wonder this stanza reflects his depression.

Depressed but not defeated! Down but not out! For at the very end of this discussion of affliction and this anxious reflection on his enemies, the psalmist nevertheless turns his attention once again to God's Word. It's like a gasping cry to God: "Preserve my life according to your love, and I will obey the statutes of your mouth" (v. 88). The ancients had a saying that went: *dum spiro spero* ("While I breathe I hope"). But here the child of God does better. He exclaims: *dum expiro spero* ("Even while I expire I hope"). He expected to be blessed.

Some of the older writers, among them Jerome and Ambrose, point out that for the ancients there was often significance in the shape of the Hebrew letters. And so here. This is the *kaph* stanza. *Kaph* is a curved letter, similar to a half circle, and it was often thought of as a hand held out to receive some gift or blessing.[6] That is a good image with which to end this chapter. The writer is in need and he knows that the only one who can answer his need is God. So he holds out his hand to God for his blessing.

That is all any of us can do. We can hold out empty hands. If we hold out hands filled with our own good works, there is no way God can fill them. Our hands will be unable to hold more; and, besides, God will not add his grace to our works. But if we hold out empty hands, God will fill them, to the praise of the glory of his great grace.

7

The Eternal Word

Your word, O LORD, is eternal;
  it stands firm in the heavens.
Your faithfulness continues through all generations;
  you established the earth, and it endures.
Your laws endure to this day,
  for all things serve you.
If your law had not been my delight,
  I would have perished in my affliction.
I will never forget your precepts,
  for by them you have preserved my life.
Save me, for I am yours;
  I have sought out your precepts.
The wicked are waiting to destroy me,
  but I will ponder your statutes.
To all perfection I see a limit;
  but your commands are boundless.

Psalm 119:89–96

PSALM 119 IS NOT OFFERED TO US SO THAT WE CAN READ OF the personal life experiences of the psalmist. It is a collection of inspired reflections on the nature of God's Word and of the righteous person's proper response to it. Nevertheless, it is hard to escape feeling that, in some places at least, the writer is speaking personally. Stanzas nine through eleven describe the psalmist's afflictions, and they do so in such a powerful and poignant way that we can hardly doubt that these were sufferings the writer actually did experience.

In moving from the *kaph* to the *lamedh* stanzas (from stanza eleven to stanza twelve), we are passing the midpoint of the psalm and are moving beyond the point where the psalmist is at his lowest. In stanza twelve we find that God has preserved and delivered the poet and as a result there is an entirely different tone in the psalm. From this point on the writer moves forward and upward, building his life on the only foundation that is truly steadfast and eternal—the enduring Word of God.

It is as if he had been struggling in a pounding ocean surf, trying desperately to reach land, and at last has drawn himself up onto a great rock on the shore. Or it is as if he had been sinking in quicksand and has suddenly found solid ground beneath his feet. That rock, that solid foundation, is the Word of God. If the psalmist had known that great hymn from the *Selection of Hymns* by Rippon (1787), he might well have sung:

> How firm a foundation, ye saints of the Lord,
> Is laid for your faith in his excellent Word!
> What more can he say than to you he hath said,
> To you who for refuge to Jesus have fled?

Actually, he has sung it (the content, if not the very words) in this stanza of Psalm 119.

God's Everlasting Word

Martin Luther once wrote of God's Word, "The Bible is alive, it speaks to me; it has feet, it runs after me; it has hands, it lays hold of me. The Bible is not antique or modern. It is eternal."[1] That is the theme of this stanza or, more particularly, of verses 89–91.

Each of these verses is more or less parallel to the others. That is, each says virtually the same thing, and what each says is that God's Word is everlasting and therefore a person can build on it, not only for this life but for eternity. Verse 89 says: "Your word, O LORD, is eternal; it stands firm in the heavens." Verse 90 says: "Your faithfulness continues through all generations; you established the earth, and it endures." Verse 91 observes: "Your laws endure to this day, for all things serve you."[2]

If "faithfulness" in verse 90 refers to God's Word, then all three verses are saying that because God's Word is eternal in heaven, it can also clearly be depended on here on earth. If "faithfulness" is being distinguished from God's Word, as a separate attribute of God, then the verses are saying that three things are eternal: (1) God's Word in heaven, (2) God's faithfulness on earth, and (3) the laws of God, which, like the heavens and the earth, endure "to this day." The laws of God will endure even longer, of course. As the last and summarizing verse of this section states: "To all perfection I see a limit; but your commands are boundless" (v. 96).

This was also the clear teaching of Jesus Christ. For example, in the Sermon on the Mount, in what is some of his most extensive teaching on this topic, Jesus said, "Do not think that I have come to abolish the Law or the Prophets; I have not come to abolish them but to fulfill them. I tell you the truth, until heaven and earth disappear, not the smallest letter, not the least stroke of a pen, will by any means disappear from the Law until everything is accomplished" (Matt. 5:17–18).

The older versions spoke of "a jot or a tittle," which was accurate but unclear to most people. That is why the New International Version expands the phrase to read "not the smallest letter, not the least stroke of a pen." Therefore, what Jesus was teaching is that not even an *i* or a *serif* of the sacred text will be lost from Scripture until every single portion of it is fulfilled. And not even then! For as he said elsewhere, "Heaven and earth will pass away, but my words will never pass away" (Matt. 24:35). The psalmist wrote, "Your word, O LORD, is eternal" (Ps. 119:89).

Neither you nor I can see things from the perspective of eternity, of course. Only God can do that. But we can testify to the enduring qualities of Scripture throughout observable history. Indeed, one reason among many for believing the Bible to be God's Word and not the word of mere human beings is its extraordinary preservation down through the centuries. Today, after the Bible has been translated, in part or whole, into many hundreds of languages, many with multiple versions, and after millions of copies have been printed and distributed, it would be nearly impossible to destroy the Bible. But this was not always so. Until the time of the Reformation—when Gutenberg's remarkable discovery of moveable type made it possible to mass reproduce and easily distribute the Bible and other literature throughout civilized lands—the text of the Bible was preserved by the laborious and time-consuming process of copying it over and over again by hand, at first onto papyrus sheets and then onto parchments. Throughout much of this time, the Bible was an object of extreme hatred by many in authority. They tried to get rid of it, but the text survived. In the early days of the church, Celsus, Prophyry, and Lucien tried to destroy it by arguments. Later the emperors Diocletian and Julian tried to destroy it by force. In some periods of history it was a capital offense to possess a copy of the Bible. Yet the text survived.

If the Bible had been only the thoughts or work of mere men, it would have been eliminated long ago, as other books have been. We know from passing references in other ancient books that we have lost masterpieces by many of the greatest writers of the past. But the Bible has endured and has endured intact. Isaiah wrote, "The grass withers and the flowers fall, but the word of our God stands forever" (Isa. 40:8).

God's Liberating Word

I have already noted several times how practical the writer of Psalm 119 is. This is a quality we see again here. His theme is the eternal or enduring character of God's Word and in this stanza he starts with that truth and then reflects on what this eternal or indestructible Word has done for him. It has done two things, he says. First, it has preserved him in his affliction. Second, it has saved and, he is sure, will continue to save him from the wicked persons who were trying to destroy him.

Preservation

Verse 92 picks up on the theme of the last three stanzas: affliction. It tells us that God heard and answered the prayer with which those stanzas end. What was it that got the psalmist through those extremely hard times? The answer, of course, is God. But that is not the way the writer states the answer in this verse. He says, "*If your law had not been my delight,* I would have perished in my affliction." In other words, what got him through his afflictions was his lifelong habit of reading, marking, learning, meditating on, inwardly digesting, and, above all, obeying God's law. Thus, even in stanza eleven, the lowest point of all in this long psalm, he maintains:

"I have put my hope in your word" (v. 81).
"I do not forget your decrees" (v. 83).
"I have not forsaken your precepts" (v. 87).
"I will obey the statutes of your mouth" (v. 88).

When we get in trouble we usually go to God for help, as the writer did. But we often stop at that point, expecting God to intervene all by himself, miraculously, without any work on our part. The psalmist was wiser than we are, for while he prayed for help, he also did what he was able and obliged to do. He studied and meditated on the Bible. He knew that it is God who must work but that God nevertheless works through means specific to our need. In the matter of lifting us out of our trouble and setting our feet on a sure foundation, the great and only indispensable means of deliverance and growth is Bible study.

Martin Luther appreciated this point, for Psalm 119:92 meant a great deal to him. The words of this verse are written in his own hand in his own Bible (1542), preserved in the Brandenburg Mark Museum in Berlin.

This is a good point at which to distinguish the four synonyms for Scripture occurring in verses 81, 83, 87, and 88. "Word" (*dabar*, v. 81) is the most general of these terms. It embraces everything that God has said in the Bible, whether law or gospel, commands or promises. "Decrees" (*huqqim*, sometimes rendered "statutes," v. 83) refers to binding rules or laws, such as those inscribed on a stone tablet—the Ten Commandments, for instance. "Precepts" (*piqqudim*, v. 87) is like our word "regulations." It is what a government official might issue after he has looked into a problem and figured out what detailed rules might resolve it. "Statutes" (*'edot*, sometimes rendered "testimonies," v. 88) pictures the Bible as God's faithful witness to his people, containing warnings of distress and judgment if the Word is disobeyed and promises of blessing and joy if it is heeded.

The point is that in his affliction the psalmist took the whole of the Bible as his and clung to it tenaciously. He knew, as the apostle Paul also knew, that "*all Scripture* is God-breathed and is useful for teaching, rebuking, correcting and training in righteousness, so that the man of God may be thoroughly equipped for every good work" (2 Tim. 3:16–17). We never know what portion of the Bible God will use to bless us and keep us steady in hard times.

Verse 93 is parallel to verse 92. In fact verses 94 and 95 are parallel too, making two statements of deliverance.

Prayers for preservation are a recurring motif in this psalm. The psalmist prayed for preservation as early as verse

25 ("preserve my life according to your word"), a sentence that he repeated word for word in verse 37. In verse 40 he wrote, "Preserve my life in your righteousness." Verse 50 declared, "Your promise preserves my life." The same thought occurs in the latter half of the psalm: verse 107 ("preserve my life, O LORD, according to your word") and again in verse 149; verse 154 ("preserve my life according to your promise"); and verse 156 ("preserve my life according to your laws"). In the twelfth stanza the psalmist is not praying for preservation, he is declaring that God *has* preserved him. But notice: the preservation came about as he remembered God's Word, which is what the other verses also affirm. "I will never forget your precepts, for by them you have preserved my life" (v. 93).

How do we think of preservation? We think of it as something God does by his Holy Spirit, which is right, of course. But we tend to forget the link between the Holy Spirit and God's Word. We must remember that the Word and the Spirit always go together, as I pointed out earlier. God *speaks to us* through both of them working together, and it is also through the Word and not apart from it that the Spirit *renews us* inwardly.

And speaking of renewal, we cannot miss noting that although affliction was the theme of the preceding three stanzas, where it was developed at great length, and although it has reoccurred in this stanza (in verse 92), it appears here only briefly and as something in the past. Why? Because God has indeed preserved the psalmist and he is no longer under that depression of spirit that his afflictions caused.

Salvation

Verses 94 and 95 belong together because they deal with salvation from the psalmist's enemies. They were part of his afflictions, because he referred to them earlier in that way: "When will you punish my persecutors?" (v. 84) and "They almost wiped me from the earth" (v. 87). God delivered him from those wicked people who were against him, renewing his life and spirits. This was truly a great salvation. But now we discover that these wicked people are still around, since "the wicked are waiting to destroy me," he says (v. 95).

This is why a third of these statements of what God has done is in the form of an ongoing prayer ("Save me") and not a statement about something in the past, as was the case with the others ("I would have perished" and "you have preserved my life"). The writer needed God's salvation constantly.

And so do we. If God were not with us every moment of every single day, sustaining our lives and preserving us from constant dangers, perceived and unperceived, we would certainly perish in an instant. But even more than this, we need God's constant salvation from our sins. We sometimes speak of three tenses of salvation: (1) There is the salvation in the past by which Jesus died for our sin, making atonement by his death, and God forgave us on the basis of that utterly sufficient atonement. (2) Salvation in the present is that by which we are enabled to grow in grace and holiness by the power of God's Spirit working through his written Word, attaining higher and higher levels of obedience and understanding. (3) Salvation in the future is when we shall be taken to heaven and delivered from the very presence of sin and from all desires to yield to it.

How can we be sure that in all three of these tenses God will save us, as we so desperately need? It is because "he who began a good work in you will carry it on to completion until the day of Christ Jesus" (Phil. 1:6). That is a promise. In other words, to go back to the theme of this stanza stated in verses 89–91, it is because the Word of God "is eternal" and "stands firm in the heavens" and because it "continues through all generations" and endures "to this day."

And look at the words "for I am yours" in verse 94. Each has only one syllable; they are simplicity itself. But what an amazing truth that we should belong to God. If we belong to him, we can count on him to save us—now and to the very end. Charles Spurgeon called verse 94 "a comprehensive prayer with a prevailing argument," noting that "if we are confident that we are the Lord's, we may be confident that he will save us."[3]

Standing on the Rock

The last verse of this section stands alone as a summary statement that links the truth that God's law is eternal (vv. 89–91) with the salvation that is ours through believing and acting on God's commands (vv. 92–95): "To all perfection I see a limit; but your commands are boundless" (v. 96).

Earlier in the stanza the poet wrote, "You established the earth, and it endures" (v. 90). He is making a connection between earthly physical laws and the eternal Word of God. But here he seems to acknowledge that even this apparently stable earth will disappear at last, as Jesus affirmed years later ("Heaven and earth will pass away," Matt. 24:35). All that is merely of this earth and merely material shall pass away. "To all perfection I see a limit" (v. 96), the writer says. But like Jesus, the psalmist also knew that there is one thing that will remain forever and that is God's Word. Jesus continued, as quoted by Matthew, "but my words will never pass away" (Matt. 24:35). The psalmist said, "But your commands are boundless."

Derek Kidner wrote of this summarizing statement, "This verse could well be a summary of Ecclesiastes, where every earthly enterprise has its day and comes to nothing, and where only in God and his commandments do we get beyond these frustrating limits."[4]

So why don't we stand on this foundation and build on it? If you wanted to build a house and had a choice between a solid rock and sand for your foundation, wouldn't you choose the solid rock? If you were investing for your retirement years and had a choice between a proven blue-chip firm and a fly-by-night over-the-counter venture, wouldn't you choose the blue-chip firm? Why, then, should you do differently with your life, which is of far greater value than a house or a bank account? Why should you not build on a foundation that will stand against life's tempests (Matt. 7:24–27)?

I like what the great Anglican Bishop John Charles Ryle said on one occasion when it was pointed out that the Bible was under attack by the so-called higher critics. Ryle said, "Give me the plenary, verbal theory of biblical inspiration with all its difficulties, rather than the doubt. I accept the difficulties and I humbly wait for their solution. But while I wait, I am standing on rock."

8

Loving God's Word

O, how I love your law!
 I meditate on it all day long.
Your commands make me wiser than my enemies,
 for they are ever with me.
I have more insight than all my teachers,
 for I meditate on your statutes.
I have more understanding than the elders,
 for I obey your precepts.
I have kept my feet from every evil path
 so that I might obey your word.
I have not departed from your laws,
 for you yourself have taught me.
How sweet are your words to my taste,
 sweeter than honey to my mouth!
I gain understanding from your precepts;
 therefore I hate every wrong path.

                                    Psalm 119:97–104

WHAT AN UPLIFTING STANZA THIS IS, THE *MEM* STANZA! IT IS
filled with joy and with love for God's law, so much so that
there is not even a single petition in it. Can this be the same
poet who was sunk in near despair just two stanzas earlier? We

know the answer, of course. It is the same person exactly, and the reason for the change is precisely that for which the poet is now praising God, namely, the Bible or God's law. The first verse sets the tone for the stanza when it declares fervently, "Oh, how I love your law! I meditate on it all day long" (v. 97).

Loving God's Written Revelation

The theme of the stanza, then, is the writer's love for the Bible. He has mentioned loving God's law before (in verses 47–48), but not as often through the psalm as we might have expected. Here it is his chief emphasis.

In his short study of the psalms, *Reflections on the Psalms,* C. S. Lewis has a chapter on the love of God's law that the various psalm writers express. He confesses how strange this seemed to him when he was starting to study the psalms. He understood how a writer could respect a good law and try to obey it. But to love it or delight in it seemed to him a bit like loving the instruments with which a dentist pulls out teeth or enjoying being on the front line of a battlefield in wartime. Part of the answer to this query is that *law* in the psalms means more than mere laws. It means the whole of God's written revelation, including promises as well as warnings, blessings as well as judgments. Yet this cannot be the whole answer, because the psalmist seems to be rejoicing in, at least in part, perhaps even emphasizing, those specific commandments of the Bible that keep him from every evil path. In other words, it is not just the promises that delight him, but the laws as well.

What Lewis came to see is that the characteristic of the law of God that the psalmists loved is what Lewis calls the engaging moral order of the divine mind, which is why Psalm 119, of all the psalms, particularly speaks of loving God's law. We think of love primarily as an emotion. But this is not a particularly emotional psalm. It is an ordered, carefully constructed psalm, reflecting in its very pattern something of what the psalmist saw in the mind of God and not only respected but loved deeply.

Lewis wrote,

> The Order of the Divine mind, embodied in the Divine Law, is beautiful. [Therefore] what should a man do but try to reproduce it, so far as possible, in his daily life? His 'delight' is in those statutes (16); to study them is like finding treasure (14); they affect him like music, are his 'songs' (54); they taste like honey (103); they are better than silver and gold (72). As one's eyes are more and more opened, one sees more and more in them, and it excites wonder (18). This is not priggery nor even scrupulosity; it is the language of a man ravished by a moral beauty. If we cannot at all share his experience, we shall be the losers.[1]

Lewis concludes by suggesting that a Chinese Christian might be able to appreciate Psalm 119 better than most westerners, because it is a part of that culture to value a life that is arranged according to a cosmic order.

In this stanza the writer gives five reasons why he has learned to love God's law and thus why we should love it too. It is because it is the source of true wisdom; it keeps us on the right path and off wrong ones; when we study it, we have God himself as our teacher; the law is sweet to our spiritual taste, like honey; and it not only keeps us from evil, it also causes us to hate every wrong path.

Wisdom from on High

The first of the psalmist's reasons for loving God's law is the one most emphasized, for it is repeated in parallel fashion three times in verses 98–100. It is that God's Word is the source of true wisdom. This is repeated so often that many scholars regard wisdom, rather than love of God's law, as the stanza's actual theme.

Like many parallel statements in the psalms, these verses have several sets of parallel ideas. As far as God's Word is concerned, the writer refers to it as: "your commands" (v. 98), "your statutes" (v. 99), and "your precepts" (v. 100). As far as wisdom is concerned, he reflects on being "wiser" (v. 98), having "more insight" (v. 99), and possessing "more understanding" than other wise people (v. 100). As far as comparisons with others who might claim to be wise are concerned, he says that the Bible has made him wiser than his "enemies" (v. 98), his "teachers" (v. 99), and "the elders" of the people (v. 100).

How can this be? How can the writer claim to be wiser than these others, particularly his teachers and the elders? Is this only the boast of some smart young student who thinks he has all the answers when he actually hardly even knows the right questions? Is he a "sophomore" in God's school, one whose initial learning has made him only a "wise moron," which is what the word "sophomore" means? In each of these comparisons the psalmist is thinking of those who appear wise by the world's standards but who lack the deeper wisdom that comes from the law of God.

This is clearest in the matter of his enemies. He has a lot to say about enemies in this psalm (as other psalm writers, especially David, also do), but he is not thinking here of the particular danger his enemies may have in store for him personally. He is thinking of their skill in manipulating truth and circumstances to their own worldly advantage. In this they are indeed shrewd. Even Jesus said, "The people of this world are more shrewd [KJV, wiser] in dealing with their own kind than are the people of the light" (Luke 16:8). But to provide for "old number one" in this way is not genuine wisdom, since at its best it is for this life only, and at its worse it is perverted and destructive. We remember how Jesus also asked, "What good will it be for a man if he gains the whole world, yet forfeits his soul?" (Matt. 16:26). It is that better, spiritual wisdom—the salvation of his soul—that the psalmist gains by love for and obedience to God's Word.

It is not that the psalmist is made wise enough to outsmart these worldly enemies on their own terms; that does not fit the tone of the psalm at all. It is rather that these people have set themselves against God's law, considering themselves to be superior to it, and the psalmist finds that he is made wiser than they are by his submission to God's commands.

How about his teachers and the elders? Again, it is not that there is nothing to be learned from one's teachers. They have accumulated knowledge. Or elders. Elders have accumulated experience. He is not saying that in general terms he has outstripped those who have studied longer or lived longer than he has. There is always much to learn from other wise people. Rather he is comparing spiritual learning with mere worldly wisdom and experience, and he is saying that the wisdom of God goes beyond anything he can learn from mere secular instructors.

And there is this too: Worldly wisdom is transient. "Where there is knowledge, it will pass away," wrote Paul (1 Cor. 13:8). The knowledge of one generation is constantly being outmoded, especially by the fast pace of modern life. But the knowledge gained from the Bible is eternal. It will be as true on the day of our death as when we first learned it.

The Path of Righteousness

The second reason the psalmist has come to love God's law is that it has kept him in the path of righteousness. It has kept him on the right path and off wrong ones. Earlier in the psalm the writer asked pointedly, "How can a young man keep his way pure?" (v. 9). He answered, "By living according to your word." He is saying the same thing now (in verse 101), but he is stating it the other way around: "I have kept my feet from every evil path so that I might obey your word." In other words, it is what one of the older evangelists wrote on the flyleaf of his Bible: "This book will keep you from sin, or sin will keep you from this book."

These verses are not saying that the best of many equally valuable ways for a young person or anyone else to keep his or her way pure is by studying God's Word. They are saying that this is the only way. And the reason for this is that only the Word of God can tell us what the pure way is. A pure or right way is the opposite of a sinful way, and knowledge of sin by definition requires a knowledge of God's law. What is sin? "Sin is any want of conformity unto or transgression of the law of God," says the *Westminster Shorter Catechism* (answer to question 14). Apart from the law of God there may still be wrong behavior, but it can only be defined as a violation of the laws of the state, which is crime, or simply offenses against humanity, which is to break the law of nature. Only the law of God can tell us what offends God, hence, what sin is. Similarly, only the law of God can show us the right path in which to walk.

Moreover, only the Word of God can empower us to do it. To be sure, the law as law does not do it. The law exposes sin and condemns the sinner. But it is also true that the Spirit works through the whole of Scripture for our good. And what the Spirit does through Scripture is revive, illumine, and empower the child of God first to believe the gospel of salvation by the work of Jesus Christ and then to live by his teachings.

God Is My Teacher

The psalmist continues with his reasons for loving God's law. He says that when he studies it, he finds God to be his teacher: "I have not departed from your laws, for you yourself have taught me" (v. 102).

In Hebrew, as in many languages, it is not necessary to have a subject pronoun with a verb because the ending of the verb indicates the subject. In this verse the ending of the verb is "you," meaning God: "You taught me." However, the verse also contains the additional separate pronoun "you," which can only be in the verse for emphasis. This is why the New International Version adds the word "yourself," saying, "for you *yourself* have taught me." This is an important point, for it means that when the writer studied the Bible, what he heard in it were not the words of other people, even though they had been used of God to record the revelation. He heard the voice of God himself. It is God who spoke to him. This is true for us as well. God speaks to us in Scripture and this makes the Bible unlike any merely human book.

When I read this verse I think of Genesis 3:8 and its reference to God "walking in the garden in the cool of the day." The verse suggests that this was God's regular pattern, that Adam and Eve used to meet God in Eden in the cool evening hours, after the work of the day was done, and that they used to converse with God and be taught by him. The reason they hid from him in Genesis 3 is not that God's coming was unusual but that they had sinned by eating of the tree of the knowledge of good and evil and were now afraid of him.

Christians sometimes imagine what those halcyon days before the fall were like, musing on how wonderful it would be to have God walk with us and talk to us in such an intimate way. We sometimes sing about it in the words of the C. Austin Miles hymn (1912), not really believing what we say:

> I come to the garden alone,
> While the dew is still on the roses;
> And the voice I hear, falling on my ear;
> The Son of God discloses.
> And He walks with me, and He talks with me,
> And He tells me I am His own,
> And the joy we share as we tarry there,
> None other has ever known.

That is a pretty sentimental piece of bad poetry, and it probably says the wrong thing to most people who sing it.

Just me and Jesus! Nobody else, no Bible! No mediated revelation! Yet there is a sense in which the psalmist says that is exactly what he finds when he studies Scripture. It takes him back to Eden, not in an unfallen state to be sure, but to a place where he is personally taught by God. And what this means for us is that, although we have forfeited Eden, we have a taste of Eden or, better yet, of heaven, when we come to the Bible and find that God himself speaks to us there.

It is this quality of Scripture that the Reformers had in mind when they said that Scripture is "self-authenticating." They meant that a true Christian does not need a church, a church council, or the pope to tell him what Scripture says, since the Bible bears on its very surface the stamp of the divine mind and is God speaking.

Sweeter Than Honey and the Honeycomb

The fourth thing the psalmist says about God's law is that it is sweet to his taste: "How sweet are your words to my taste, sweeter than honey to my mouth!" (v. 103).

This is almost exactly what David wrote in Psalm 19:10, which shows that the writer of our later psalm must have been acquainted with the earlier one. David had written that God's ordinances "are sweeter than honey, than honey from the comb."

How are we to think (or talk) about the Bible being sweet? We hardly think of anything being sweet except certain kinds of food, like sugar donuts, Godiva chocolates, or honey. But even if we did think of other things as being sweet, it is hard to think of God's Word or laws in this way. This is the puzzle that C. S. Lewis was wrestling with. Do we ever think of the Scriptures being sweet? Do we even know what that means?

One place we might start in trying to get some understanding is by noting that what the psalmist says is sweet are the "promises" or "sayings" (plural) of God. This might mean that what he is thinking about is not the whole of God's book, considered as a gigantic block of revelation, but of individual verses that he has learned, that are turning around in his head and, yes, to use the phrase of the well-known Anglican collect, that he is trying to "inwardly digest." No one is able to take it all in, to master the Bible as a whole. But what the writer was able to do, and commends to us, is to take the specific sayings of God and learn to love them one by one.

This is a hard matter to get across, first, because most of us do not love the words of God like this and therefore do not know what someone who really loves them is talking about, and second, because this is a personal matter even for those who do love God's Word, and different verses have spoken and will continue to speak to different people. But let me try to give the flavor of it.

Take the Twenty-third Psalm as an example. Many people love it because of the beautiful picture it paints of God as our loving, caring, and ever faithful Shepherd. I love all kinds of poetry, but I confess that there is something exquisite about the shepherd image in this psalm. Is anything more beautiful than this? More sweet to the taste?

> The LORD is my shepherd, I shall not be in want.
>   He makes me lie down in green pastures,
> he leads me beside quiet waters,
>   he restores my soul.

I am sure the psalmist knew the truth of these verses and turned it over and over again both in his mind and on his tongue. So should we. If we can't find anything beautiful or sweet in those words, our taste buds are terribly dulled and our eyes horribly glazed over by the tawdry glitz of our culture.

Or how about this? "O LORD, our Lord, how majestic is your name in all the earth!" (Psalm 8:1 and 9). That comes from my favorite psalm. I think every syllable of that great psalm is a treasure.

Or think of John 3:16 or Romans 8:28 or Romans 11:32–36 or the very last promise of the Bible, Revelation 22:20: "He who testifies to these things says, 'Yes, I am coming soon.'" And our response to it: "Amen. Come, Lord Jesus." We live in a garish, loud, mean, harsh, strident, ugly, and abusive age. Don't you find it sweet to turn aside from all that, at least from time to time, and fill your heart with something really beautiful? If you have never done it, why don't you try? Try memorizing some particularly delightful portions of Scripture. You will find that it will make you a bit more delightful too. It will soothe the bitter experiences of life with God's sweetness, the ugly things with God's beauty, and sadness with joy.

Hating Every Wrong Path

The Christian life is not all sweetness, however. To say that would be to sentimentalize it. It has its sweet moments, and there is great beauty in God, but we still live in a sour, ugly world. It is important that we learn to hate evil as well as love the good. That is the fifth thing the psalmist says God did for him through his study of the Bible and why he came to love God's law: "I gain understanding from your precepts; therefore I hate every wrong path" (v. 104).

Isn't it interesting that the psalmist ends on this note. It is the exact opposite of how the stanza began. It began with love: "Oh, how I love your law." It ends with hate: "Therefore I hate every wrong path." Does that seem strange to you? Offensive? Absurd?

It is not absurd, because we never learn that anything is truly good unless we also learn that its opposite is not good and we turn from it. "Attraction to the true and revulsion against the false are . . . acquired tastes," says Derek Kidner.[2] Discrimination is the only real test of wisdom, and hatred of evil is the ultimate proof that we love God.

Loving God's Word

Are you indifferent to the Bible? Do you find it boring, unattractive? If so, you will not be kept from sin or from what is evil and offensive in this world. You will make your home in it. Don't do that. Instead, read, study, learn, and meditate on God's Word and you will find that it grows sweeter and sweeter to your taste. And, equally important, you will learn that sin is to be avoided at all costs.

9

The Clarity of God's Word

Your word is a lamp to my feet
    and a light for my path.
I have taken an oath and confirmed it,
    that I will follow your righteous laws.
I have suffered much;
    preserve my life, O LORD, according to your word.
Accept, O LORD, the willing praise of my mouth,
    and teach me your laws.
Though I constantly take my life in my hands,
    I will not forget your law.
The wicked have set a snare for me,
    but I have not strayed from your precepts.
Your statutes are my heritage forever;
    they are the joy of my heart.
My heart is set on keeping your decrees
    to the very end.

Psalm 119:105–12

THE NIGHTTIME JOURNEYS OF ISRAEL THROUGH THE WILDER-
ness were illumined by a pillar of fire that moved before them
on their march. Most of the time the pillar stood in the center of their camp over the Most Holy Place of the taberna-

cle where during the day it was a pillar of cloud. But when they marched, it went before them to lead the way, and at night, as a flaming pillar of light, it also illumined their path (see Exodus 40:36–38).[1] In a similar way our nighttime passage through the dark and dangerous journey of this life is illumined by God's Word, the Bible. That is how stanza fourteen, the *nun* stanza, of Psalm 119 begins: "Your word is a lamp to my feet and a light for my path" (v. 105).

In his commentary Alexander Maclaren comments on the fact that God's Word is pictured both as a lamp and a light. "A lamp is for night; light shines in the day," he says. "The Word is both to the psalmist." This antithesis may mean that the Law gives "light of every sort" or in all "the varying phases of experience."[2] It is a light for our darkness and for our brighter times as well.

The place to begin this study is by noting the clarity of Scripture, that attribute of the Bible that meant so much to the Protestant reformers, who also called it perspicuity. What they meant by *clarity* or *perspicuity* is that the Bible is basically clear, lucid, or comprehensible to any open-minded person who reads it. Therefore it does not require an ordained clergyman or official church magisterium to tell the typical believer in the church what it means. That is not to say that all parts of the Bible are equally clear or that there are no difficult passages. It does not mean that there is no value in an educated clergy or in acquiring some knowledge of the accumulated wisdom of the church. The creeds, catechisms, confessions, and theologies of the church are valuable for digesting and remembering what the Bible teaches. A serious student of the Bible is foolish to neglect them.

Even more, the clarity of the Bible is not an excuse for supporting merely private opinion—what the Bible means to me—as if any harebrained notion of the Bible's teaching is to be thought as valid as any other. In fact *perspicuity* means exactly the opposite. It means that the Bible is sufficiently clear so that anyone can read it and discover what the Bible is saying.

Why then are there so many differing theologies in the church? There are two answers to this. One is that we are sinners who have a built-in tendency to misread and misinterpret the Bible to our personal advantage, seeing its teaching through our own distorted grids. This is not unique to our reading the Bible. We have a tendency to do this with anything at all. We rework the simplest facts to put ourselves in a good light and other people in the wrong. That is why cultures develop elaborate legal systems to try to get to the heart of disputed matters. It is also why we must pray when we study the Bible, asking God to keep our sinful, self-serving biases from getting in the way. It is also why we use the work of believers from the past, drawing on the wisdom others had before us.

The other answer is that in spite of our sinful distortions of God's Word, there is far more agreement among Christians on what the Bible teaches than the objection assumes. In spite of our many divisions, some of them hardened by centuries of ecclesiastical disputes and warfare, there is still agreement among true Christians on most essentials of the Bible's teaching. We believe in a trinitarian God, the full deity and full humanity of Jesus Christ, the reality of our sin, Jesus' vicarious death in our place for sin so that we might be saved from it, the work of the Holy Spirit in leading us to faith, the church, the moral law of God, the return of Christ, the resurrection of the dead, and the final judgment. That is only a quick overview of Christian theology but it is a lot. It is basically what is expressed well in the ecumenical creeds: the Apostles' Creed, the Nicene Creed, and others.

Light on Our Dark Path

This fourteenth stanza speaks of the clarity of the Word of God, but the Bible is not only clear itself; it is clarifying, which means that we see other things clearly by its light. The writer of the psalm identifies some of these things: the way we should go (v. 105), righteous behavior (v. 106), suffering (v. 107), right worship (v. 108), the dangers of this life (v. 109), enemies (v. 110), and our heritage (v. 111). Therefore he says, "My heart is set on keeping your decrees to the very end" (v. 112).

The Way We Should Go

The Word of God clarifies the way we should go or—another way of saying the same thing—the way we should live our lives. It is what verse 105 is talking about when it calls God's Word "a lamp to my feet and a light for my path." We do not know how to live our lives, but the Bible shines light on the path before us to expose the wrong, dangerous ways we might take and to light up the right ones.

On this point many Christians have a wrong idea of how the Bible works. They suppose it exists to give them detailed instructions concerning the choices in life: what job they should take, whom they should marry, where they should live, how they should spend their vacations, and so on. This is not how the Word of God functions. It does not offer special or mystical leading. It reveals the kind of character a Christian should have and shows the priorities that should govern his or her thinking. This is true light on our path and it is only the Bible that provides it. Nothing in the world provides us the same illumination. On the contrary, the world always sets the wrong priorities and extols perverted character.

Righteous Behavior

Verse 106 is not talking about the righteousness of God that is imputed to us through faith in Jesus Christ. It is concerned with righteous actions, which is why it speaks of following God's "righteous laws." Why do we need the Bible to know what is right and wrong? Doesn't the world have an intrinsic sense of right and wrong that enables governments to enact good laws? Don't people have a conscience that helps them know what is good and what is not? The answer to these questions is yes, to a point. There is such a thing as natural law, which provides a moral foundation common to human beings almost everywhere. Generally people know that it is wrong to kill, steal, lie, and dishonor parents, for instance.

But these are not the areas in which we have our greatest problems. If a choice is black and white, we know what to do. Unfortunately the problems we face are usually not black and white but gray. We suspect we should do one thing, but there is another side to it. And if the situation does not seem gray to us immediately, if we talk to our friends, it becomes gray soon enough, since everyone sees it from a different point of view. How are we to find our way through the gray landscape of life? There is only one way, and that is by studying, meditating on, and seeking to apply the Bible to our lives. The Bible is not gray. There are things in it we may not fully understand, but when we do understand what the Bible teaches, which is often enough, it is very clear. Thus the Bible is a light for our moral path. The path is dark because the world is dark, but the Bible clarifies the issues and shows us how to walk through the darkness.

Suffering

Verse 107 speaks of suffering. "I have suffered much," says the psalmist. Does the Bible help here? One thing it does is explain the various reasons for suffering. We saw this earlier in verses 65–88. Nothing but God's Word can show us that some suffering is merely common to man, some corrective, still other suffering constructive, Christ-glorifying, or even cosmic.

But that is not what the psalmist is talking about in this particular verse, for what follows is the prayer "preserve my life . . . according to your word." This means that in his suffering the writer turned to the Bible and found God to be present in its pages, promising a renewal of his life and spirit when he would go through hard times. It was God's presence and God's promises that kept him going. If ever there was a light on his dark path, it was then. If ever there was a light at the end of his dark tunnel, it was when he opened the Bible's pages.

Right Worship

In verse 108 the psalmist speaks of two things that go together: praising God with his mouth and being taught God's laws. These belong together because they are what right worship and the practice of true religion are all about.

To put it another way, they are what ought to go on in church. What should happen when we come to church? First and most important, we should be taught the Bible. God has spoken in the Bible and it is in the Bible that he continues to speak. There is nothing more important for Christian growth and the health of the church than sound Bible teaching. Yet sadly, serious Bible teaching is widely neglected in our day, even in so-called evangelical churches. Instead of Bible teaching, people are being fed a diet of superficial pop psychology, self-help therapy, feel-good stimulants, and entertainment. The ignorance of the Bible in the churches is appalling. George Gallup has followed the rise of biblical illiteracy for decades and he reports that, although Americans revere the Bible highly—almost every home in America has a Bible and most people say they believe it—only small percentages know who preached the Sermon on the Mount, are able to name the four gospels, or can recall even one of the Ten Commandments.

Not long ago the staff of CURE (Christians United for Reformation) was at the National Christian Booksellers Convention and conducted an informal survey to determine if people there could name the Ten Commandments. Shane Rosenthal, the producer of CURE's radio program, the White Horse Inn, asked 256 people if they could name the Ten Commandments just off the top of their heads. In that huge assembly, not of secular people but of evangelical staff persons and leaders, only one person could do it. And these are people who are lobbying to get the Ten Commandments restored to the walls of our courtrooms and the public schools!

The other element of religion mentioned in this verse is the "willing praise" of God with our mouths. We praise God whenever we speak of him gratefully, of course, but it is natural in this context to think of how we praise God by singing. Do we praise him? There is much emotional music and frequently repeated words and slogans. But one thing I notice as I travel around the country speaking in evangelical churches is the loss of the great hymns of Christianity. This might be all right if the church's hymns were being replaced by better ones, but the new hymns are not better. They are usually trite, theologically vacuous, man-centered, and simply misleading.

All this goes along with our pitiful ignorance of the Bible, and it will not be corrected until we recover some biblical depth. If we knew the Bible, it would expose our bad practices, enable us to correct them quickly, and draw us again to a true biblical worship of God. We cannot know what might please God in our worship unless we find it in Scripture.

The Dangers of This Life

The Hebrew of verse 109 says literally, "My soul in my hands constantly." The idea is exactly the same as the English idiom, "I am taking my life in my hands." It means that the writer is in constant danger.

Whenever we find the psalms talking about danger, we usually think of physical danger, and it is true that the psalmists, particularly David, did face physical danger. David's enemies were usually out to kill him. But this is not all the psalms speak of. They also speak of spiritual dangers like falling into sin or forgetting God. This verse combines these two ideas. When the writer speaks of taking his life in his hands, he is expressing the idea of actually losing it. That is, he might be killed. But when he adds, nevertheless, "I will not forget your law," he is confessing that the far greater danger would be for him to abandon God's Word and begin to live a purely secular life. In other words, the Bible clarifies the nature of the danger and shows where his true peril lies.

Do we understand that about life? I do not think so, and evidence of that is the nature of our prayers. The prayers I hear have to do almost exclusively with having good health (or getting better when we or someone else is sick), succeeding at our jobs, passing a test, or perhaps praying that someone else might become a Christian. But where are the prayers that we might be kept from sin, that we or those close to us might become more godly, that we might be able to live better for God or get to know God better? We need the Bible to clarify our true danger. We will never be aware of our danger without it.

Enemies

Verse 110 teaches the same lessons as verse 109, making clear that the writer really was in danger of being killed by his enemies. They are "the wicked" who had set snares for him. If we are trying to live for Christ, we will have similar experiences. Ungodly people will also set snares for us because they hate us and the Lord we are serving. They will try to make us look bad before our friends or fail at our jobs. If we are going to see our way through this problem and remain on the right path spiritually, we are going to have to study God's Word to get our priorities straight and be reminded that it is far more important to be approved by God than by other people.

But how can we read of wicked people fixing snares for us without thinking also of our even greater enemy, the devil, who, we are told, is "crafty" (Gen. 3:1), "the father of lies" (John 8:44) and "like a roaring lion looking for someone to devour" (1 Peter 5:8). If we are going to triumph over this most terrible enemy, we will need to know everything the Bible says about him and his tactics. We will need to know that he is powerful, but also that he is a defeated foe. Most important of all, we will need to know that the greatest battles we face are "not against flesh and blood [that is, what other people might do], but against . . . the spiritual forces of evil in the heavenly realms" (Eph. 6:12). The Bible clarifies the nature of these struggles, showing that it is our spiritual battles, rather than mere material or physical success, that really matter.

The Believer's True Heritage

Our spiritual battles lead to our spiritual heritage; that is what we are looking to and working for. What do you suppose that is? Will the writer say that his heritage is some heavenly reward? A golden crown perhaps, or a palace? A word of praise from God? Surprisingly, he says that his heritage is what he has been speaking about all along—God's Word. "Your statutes are my heritage forever; they are the joy of my heart" (v. 111).

What a remarkable statement! Why does he say that all he desires for his inheritance is what he already possesses? Why should *we* say it?

There are several reasons.

First, of all the many seemingly weighty and important things we know on this earth, the only thing that will last forever is God's Word. We saw this earlier when dealing with verse 96. Jesus was not exaggerating when he said, "Heaven and earth will pass away but my words will never pass away" (Matt. 24:35). Our houses will pass away. Our bank accounts will pass away. Our earthly achievements and reputations will pass away. Everything that is part of this material world will pass away. Only the Word of God will not. It makes sense that the psalmist would fix his mind on God's Word and cherish it.

Second, because the law of God is the very Word of God, it is actually part of God himself, just as our words are part of who we are. In fact his Word is what we possess of God here on earth. So when the writer says that God's statutes are his heritage forever, what he is actually saying is that God himself is his heritage. He said it explicitly earlier: "You are my portion, O LORD" (v. 57). There is nothing better than that. So he does not look for anything better. How could he? He sets his heart on God's Word.

Third, the psalmist has found God's statutes to be "the joy of [his] heart." He is fully satisfied with God's law. Therefore he wants nothing more than to go on enjoying God's words forever. Isn't it true that the reason so many of us are dissatisfied with life is that we have not found the satisfaction in God and his Word that the psalmist has? He was spiritually rich. By contrast, we are rich in material things but poor in soul.

Persevering to the Very End

In the ending of the *nun* stanza, we see again that the psalmist was a practical person. The last statement is one of fierce determination: "My heart is set on keeping your decrees to the very end" (v. 112). The reasons he will keep God's decrees to the very end are those he has identified in this stanza. He wants to keep God's decrees because he will be able to live a God-pleasing life, he will understand the nature of true righteousness, he will possess a divine perspective on suffering and will triumph in it, he will be able to worship God rightly, he will not be turned aside from obedience to God's law by any physical danger, he will not be distracted by the snares of evil men, and he will have a heritage that will last forever.

Sometimes we talk about having a biblical worldview, as opposed to having a secular worldview. A secular worldview is bounded by what we can see and by the here and now. A biblical worldview sees everything in the light of God and from the perspective of God's revelation. This can be expressed in many ways, but there is probably no better short statement of what is involved than the content of these eight verses. They deal with God, life, righteousness, suffering, enemies, and our heritage. They are what life is about. The only reason the psalmist has attained this perspective is because the Word of God articulates it clearly.

The evangelical church needs to recapture this in our day. It needs to turn from its sad worldliness and once again begin to live by the truths of God's Word. This radical reorientation must begin with us.

10

Walking by God's Word

I hate double-minded men,
  but I love your law.
You are my refuge and my shield;
  I have put my hope in your word.
Away from me, you evildoers,
  that I may keep the commands of my God!
Sustain me according to your promise, and I will live;
  do not let my hopes be dashed.
Uphold me, and I will be delivered;
  I will always have regard for your decrees.
You reject all who stray from your decrees,
  for their deceitfulness is in vain.
All the wicked of the earth you discard like dross;
  therefore I love your statutes.
My flesh trembles in fear of you;
  I stand in awe of your laws.

I have done what is righteous and just;
  do not leave me to my oppressors.
Ensure your servant's well-being;
  let not the arrogant oppress me.
My eyes fail, looking for your salvation,

looking for your righteous promise.
Deal with your servant according to your love
   and teach me your decrees.
I am your servant; give me discernment
   that I may understand your statutes.
It is time for you to act, O LORD;
   your law is being broken.
Because I love your commands
   more than gold, more than pure gold,
and because I consider all your precepts right,
   I hate every wrong path.

Psalm 119:113–28

HAVE YOU EVER NOTICED HOW NOVELISTS DESCRIBE THE WAY a person walks to highlight his or her character? Proud men walk with their heads held high. Beautiful women glide or float. Evil villains slouch, sneak, creep, or swagger. The need to describe different ways of walking has enriched our language. *The Oxford Thesaurus* lists dozens of synonyms for walk: trek, shuffle, ramble, march, roam, wander, and others. But English is not the best of the world's languages in this respect. According to Eugene A. Nida of the American Bible Society, the Zulu language has at least 120 words for walking: to walk pompously, to walk with a swagger, to walk crouched down as when hunting a wild animal, to walk in tight clothes, and so on.

How should Christians walk? The Bible tells us to walk worthy of our "vocation" (Eph. 4:1 KJV), "uprightly" (Isa. 57:2), and "in the light" (1 John 1:7). Micah 6:8 says, "What does the LORD require of you? To act justly and to love mercy and to walk humbly with your God."

In the section of Psalm 119 to which we come now (the *samekh* and *ayin* stanzas, vv. 113–28) the writer is concerned with his walk, and the burden of his concern is that it be according to God's Word. This important theme was actually in-

114

troduced a stanza before this, with the *nun* stanza (vv. 105–12), beginning with the words: "Your word is a lamp to my feet and a light for my path" (v. 105). We looked at those words in terms of the Bible's clarity. Yet they also have to do with walking along a right path. This is the theme that continues through verse 128, which wraps up this line of thought by stating, "I hate every wrong path."

Seeing the Right Path Clearly

In regard to the believer's walk, the point of stanza fourteen is that if we are to walk as God wants us to walk, we must be able to see the right way clearly. We will never be able to see it by ourselves because this is a dark world, we have no natural light in ourselves, and there are deviating paths. We can only see the right path if the Word of God shines on it and lights it up for us. The Bible does this. It teaches us the way we should go and actually enables us to walk in it.

This stanza has two ideas in regard to walking, one positive and the other negative. As far as the positive idea is concerned, the psalmist says that he has taken an oath to "follow your righteous laws" (v. 106). That is, he has determined to obey the Bible's teaching. The Bible shows him the right path to follow. The negative idea is in verse 110: "The wicked have set a snare for me, but I have not strayed from your precepts." I think here of the apostle Paul's instruction to Timothy. In 2 Timothy chapter three he warns Timothy of "terrible times in the last days," noting that the world will be filled with vices. "People will be lovers of themselves, lovers of money, boastful, proud, abusive, disobedient to their parents, ungrateful, unholy, without love, unforgiving, slanderous, without self-control, brutal, not lovers of the good, treacherous, rash, conceited, lovers of pleasure rather than lovers of God." This is an apt description of the kind of world we live in. But what is even worse is that these vices will be in the church, for they will exist in those who have "a form of godliness" but deny "its power" (vv. 1–5).

What is Timothy to do in such terrible times? How can he keep to the right path and avoid falling into the snares that will be set for him by the wicked? He must continue in what he has learned from the Bible. The Bible is not like other books. It is God's book, and it alone will make his way plain. Paul explains it like this. "All Scripture is God-breathed and is useful for teaching, rebuking, correcting and training in righteousness, so that the man of God may be thoroughly equipped for every good work" (vv. 16–17).

There are those positive and negative points again, both of which are necessary. Teaching and training are the positive terms. Rebuking and correcting are the negatives. We need both if we are to walk in the right path and avoid the wrong ones.

Choosing Right and Rejecting Wrong

Choosing the right path and avoiding wrong ones brings us to the second stanza (vv. 113–20) in which the writer speaks particularly about right and wrong paths. The last stanza taught that the Bible alone enables us to see the right way clearly. This stanza teaches that there are many contrary paths and much opposition and if we are to walk as God wants us to walk, we must have determination.

Alexander Maclaren wrote that "this section is mainly the expression of firm resolve to cleave to the Law." He saw a meaningful outline in it. Verses 113–15 "breathe love and determination." This passes in verses 116 and 117 into "prayer in view of the psalmist's weakness and the strength of temptation." Finally, in verses 118–20 "the fate of the despisers of the Law intensifies the psalmist's clinging grasp of awe-struck love."[1] It will be helpful to follow Maclaren's outline.

Determination to Obey God's Law

How are you and I ever going to keep on obeying God's law in a sinfully enticing world like ours? There are several answers to this question. The psalm itself elaborates on quite a few of them. But one thing is certain: We are never going to obey God's law unless, from the very beginning, we determine to obey it. That is our starting point. If we are to live for God, we must determine to obey him regardless of any enticing calls to sin.

What is our chief problem in this area? The biggest problem we face is suggested in verse 113, where the writer declares, "I hate double-minded men." The adjective "double-minded" is from the same root as the word that is translated "two opinions" in 1 Kings 18:21. In that chapter Elijah is on Mount Carmel challenging the people of Israel to follow Jehovah rather than the false god Baal. "How long will you waver between two opinions? If the LORD is God, follow him; but if Baal is God, follow him," he says. Double-minded people are people who know about God but are not fully determined to worship and serve him only. Or to put it in other words, they are those who want both God and the world. They want the benefits of true religion, but they want their sin too.

The psalmist says that he hates people who are like this. He hates people halting between two opinions as much as he loves God's law. But isn't it also true that he is saying that he hates this same double-mindedness when he finds it in himself? Otherwise, why does he continue by asking God to "sustain" him, according to his promise, and "uphold" him so that he might be kept from sin? These verses "breathe" love of God's law and determination to avoid double-mindedness, as Maclaren says. But only against the dark background of his tendency to be lukewarm does this strong fixing of his mind and will to obey God's law make sense.

How about us? If the psalmist needed to fix his mind on obeying God's law, don't we also need to fix our minds on obeying God's law? James expressed this when he urged his readers to pray in faith, not wavering through any kind of indecision and doubt. The one who wavers "should not think he will receive anything from the Lord; he is a double-minded man, unstable in all he does," is what he says (James 1:7–8). Unfortunately it's true that we often do not pray in faith. We *do* waver, and the love of the world and its pleasures draws us away from God's Word.

Yet the situation is not hopeless. In fact there is great ground for confidence. Our confidence is in God, who is not double-minded and who is on the believer's side. Two points call for special notice. First, the writer calls God "my refuge and my shield" (v. 114). God is our refuge from those who would harm us, and our shield against temptations.

Second, he refers to "my God" (v. 115). This is the only place in the psalm where these words occur, but they are all the more striking for that fact. They are important because they highlight a double grip, on the one hand, the writer's grip on God and, on the other, God's grip on him. It is a case of what we call the perseverance of the saints. It's a double persevering—on God's side and ours. The saints must persevere, and will. But the reason they are able to do so is that God first of all perseveres with them.

Prayer for God's Grace

If we persevere because God first of all perseveres with us, then we need to look to him for sustaining grace to walk on the path he has set before us. This means that we must ask for God's help. It is what the psalmist does next (in verses 116–17). He prays, "Sustain me according to your promise, and I will live; do not let my hopes be dashed. Uphold me, and I will be delivered."

An interesting sidelight on this text is that in the Middle Ages, under the monastic order of the Benedictines, when a novice's period of preparation was ended and he was ready to become attached to the monastery for life, there was an induction ceremony in which, with outstretched arms, the novice recited Psalm 119:116 three times: "Sustain me according to your promise, and I will live; do not let my hopes be dashed." The community repeated the words and then sang the *Gloria Patri*, which was a way of acknowledging that the commitments of the monastic life could only be sustained by God to whom all glory belongs.[2] So too with the life of any Christian. If we are to read, study, understand, and actually obey God's Word, it will only be by God's grace, as he helps us to do it. We must get into the habit of often asking him for that help.

Standing in Awe of God

In the last three verses of this stanza the psalmist expresses a reordered outlook on the world and God, doubtless growing out of his times of prayer. He has understood his inability to obey God's law. He has sought God's help. Now having been with God, he sees afresh the deceitful vanity or emptiness of the world and the greatness of God before whom he now trembles in reverential awe.

He sees the emptiness of the world and the greatness of God at the same time. It is only when we tremble before the exalted and holy God that we are able to see the world as it really is: twisted and empty. If we do not tremble before God, the world's system seems wonderful to us and pleasantly consumes us.

Verse 120 should be read carefully, prayerfully, and with repentance by every Christian, particularly by evangelical Christians of our day. It is speaking of a reverent awe of God, an important element of walking uprightly before him. There is very little spirit of awe in our time. Instead of being in awe before God, many Christians in our day seem to regard him more as a buddy, which shows only that we do not know much about God at all. Doesn't that explain why there is so little truly godly conduct and why Christians are so much like the world? In his classical treatment of the weaknesses of the contemporary evangelical church, *No Place for Truth,*

David F. Wells speaks of the weightlessness of God, meaning that God seems to have very little bearing on the actual life of today's Christians. They do not disbelieve in him; they are Christians, after all. But he is remote from their thinking. He just doesn't enter into their everyday life.[3]

In a fascinating essay the English writer William Hazlitt (1778–1830) describes an evening in which various literary figures of his day discussed people from the past they wished they had seen. They suggested almost every great person one might think of: Homer, Dante, Shakespeare, Columbus, Caesar, Napoleon, even the American theologian Jonathan Edwards. But Charles Lamb had the last word: "There is only one other person I can ever think of after this," he said. "If Shakespeare was to come into the room, we should all rise up to meet him; but if that person [he meant Jesus] was to come into it, we should all fall down and try to kiss the hem of his garment!"[4]

That is not nearly reverence enough but it gets at the idea. Today many would merely cry out, "Hey, Jesus, come on over here and tell us how it's goin'." The psalmist says that he trembled before God and stood in awe of his laws, which is why he was a godly person and why he has been able to give us the profound teaching we have from him in this psalm.

Looking for God's Deliverance

In the *ayin* stanza (vv. 121–28), the last of the three stanzas that have to do with walking by God's Word, the contrasts that have already been introduced reoccur: the need for clear direction in a sin-dark world, the threat of enemies versus the sustaining grace of God, and hatred of sin versus love of God's Word. This stanza flows naturally from the thought that ends the last stanza: the writer's awe of God. This new stanza emphasizes that if we are to walk as God wants us to walk, we must keep looking to him intently and at all times. As far as sin is concerned, we must look to God's commandments. As far as dangers go, we must look to God for deliverance.

One combination of words that seems to tie the stanza together is "your servant," which is found in verses 122, 124, and 125. These words present the psalmist as God's servant in contrast to those who are God's enemies and who are therefore naturally oppressing him. The writer has spoken of these enemies earlier. They are the wicked of stanza fourteen, who have set snares for him (v. 110), the double-minded persons, evildoers, and wicked of the earth of stanza fifteen, whom he has turned his back on to follow after God (vv. 113, 115, 119). In stanza sixteen they are said to be oppressing him, so much so and for so long that his eyes have failed, looking for God's salvation. He needs deliverance. Therefore he is going to keep on looking to God until help comes.

According to the Massoretes, verse 122 is the only verse in the psalm that does not mention the Word of God. We have seen that verse 84 also seems not to mention it; verses 90, 121, and 132 may be examples too. But the fact that the Bible is not mentioned here, in verse 122, may be an indication of the depth of mental anguish to which the psalmist fell as a result of the oppression he had endured from wicked men. For a moment his eyes seem to be off the Bible and on his fierce oppressors instead.

But not for long! He is God's servant, and "as the eyes of slaves look to the hand of their master" and "as the eyes of a maid look to the hand of her mistress" (Ps. 123:2), so does he look up anxiously to God, expecting God to act. This stanza gives three arguments for why God should listen to his prayers and save him.

1. *Because God is a loving God* (v. 124). He has learned that God is not an indifferent, unconcerned deity. He is a loving God; that is why he has given us the Bible. Since he is a loving God, we can expect him to care for those he loves and deliver them.

121

2. *Because the writer is God's servant* (v. 125). Masters normally value those who are part of their households. If that is true on earth, shouldn't it also be true in heaven? Can God be any less caring than a good earthly master?

3. *Because it is time for God to act* (v. 126). We might expect the writer to have said that God should act now because if he delays, it will be too late; he will be crushed by his oppressors. This argument is found in other psalms.[5] But this is not what the psalmist says here. Instead of pleading his own desperate condition, he calls on God to act because "your law is being broken." How interesting! Because he is God's servant, he is more concerned with God's name and God's law than with himself and his own perilous condition.

The last two verses of this section repeat a point we saw in verse 113, namely, hatred of what is wrong contrasted with a love of what is good.

> Because I love your commands
> more than gold, more than pure gold,
> and because I consider all your precepts right,
> I hate every wrong path.
>
> verses 127–28

We live in days when it is hard for people, even alleged Christians, to accept the idea that a wrong path should be "hated." Our age is being described as postmodernity, a time in history when all things are regarded as true in the Hegelian sense; that is, they may be true for you or me or for now, but not that they have any binding validity for others or for all times; and nothing is to be considered false. Since there are no absolutes, there is nothing we can call "not true." To call it "not true" is an inexcusable power play on our part. All ways of life must be equally valid and the only thing that is absolutely wrong is to say that the path taken by someone else is wrong. It is absolutely intolerable to hate it. The time is probably coming when Christians holding to absolute standards will be considered criminals.

But Christians *do* hold to absolutes and *must* hold to them. For we know that we cannot love God and Satan too. We cannot hold to God's standards without separating from the contrary standards of the world. We cannot love the right path without hating the wrong ones. Jesus put it this way: "No one can serve two masters. Either he will hate the one and love the other, or he will be devoted to the one and despise the other. You cannot serve both God and Money" (Matt. 6:24).

Are you willing to hate what God hates? If not, you will never learn truly to love God, and you will certainly never walk in the way that brings true blessing. If you are hesitating, may I encourage you to read the first psalm in the Psalter once again. It contrasts the way of the wicked with the way of the godly. The former "*walk* in the counsel of the wicked," "*stand* in the way of sinners," and "*sit* in the seat of mockers" (Ps. 1:1, italics mine). By contrast, the godly "delight . . . in the law of the LORD" and meditate on it "day and night" (v. 2), as a result of which, they are like well-nourished trees, which yield good fruit in their season (v. 3). The psalm ends by observing, "For the LORD watches over the way of the righteous, but the way of the wicked will perish" (v. 6).

11

God's Wonderful Words

Your statutes are wonderful;
   therefore I obey them.
The unfolding of your words gives light;
   it gives understanding to the simple.
I open my mouth and pant,
   longing for your commands.
Turn to me and have mercy on me,
   as you always do to those who love your name.
Direct my footsteps according to your word;
   let no sin rule over me.
Redeem me from the oppression of men,
   that I may obey your precepts.
Make your face shine upon your servant
   and teach me your decrees.
Streams of tears flow from my eyes,
   for your law is not obeyed.

Righteous are you, O LORD,
   and your laws are right.
The statutes you have laid down are righteous;
   they are fully trustworthy.
My zeal wears me out,

for my enemies ignore your words.
Your promises have been thoroughly tested,
and your servant loves them.
Though I am lowly and despised,
I do not forget your precepts.
Your righteousness is everlasting
and your law is true.
Trouble and distress have come upon me,
but your commands are my delight.
Your statutes are forever right;
give me understanding that I may live.

Psalm 119:129–44

MANY GOOD THINGS FROM THE PAST ARE DISAPPEARING IN today's modern and postmodern society, and one of them is wonder. People used to have their sense of awe incited by some new or unexpected thing. They had expressions like "wonder-worker," "seven-day wonder" and "wonders never cease." They read books like *Alice's Adventures in Wonderland* or watched movies like *It's a Wonderful Life*. Nothing seems wonderful anymore. There is no mystery in anything. Everything seems commonplace, predictable, dull.

One reason for this is technology, which gives the impression that all reality is explicable and everything we can imagine can be done. People used to be amazed at the latest scientific inventions. They are not amazed anymore. Television has helped to take away our wonder. Television programming has an insatiable appetite for new material. Everything that can possibly be analyzed, discussed, or exploited is, including the most personal of human experiences—and at every hour of the day and night. About fifteen years ago Neil Postman wrote *The Disappearance of Childhood*, which argued that television, more than anything else, robs childhood of its lovely and appealing qualities, including, we assume, a sense of wonder at the unexpected, unexplained, and surprising beauties of life.[1]

Yet the real cause of our loss of awe is not technology or television. It is loss of an awareness of God, who alone is truly wonderful and the source of every other "wonder." If God goes, all that is genuinely wonderful goes with him.

In preparing to write this chapter, I looked in dictionaries of quotations for what people over time have said about wonder or wonderful things and I noticed that a large percentage of the quotations come from the Bible, the Book of Common Prayer, or from writers who were intentionally echoing the Bible's language. Richard Crashaw (1612–1648) wrote:

> Welcome, all wonders in one sight!
> Eternity shut in a span,
> Summer in winter, day in night,
> Heaven in earth, and God in man.
> Blest little one, whose all embracing birth
> Lifts earth to heaven, stoops heaven to earth.
> "Hymn to the Nativity"

That stanza rightly and beautifully recognizes that the greatest wonder of all is Jesus Christ and that all true wonders flow from him.

The Bible speaks of signs and wonders (see 2 Cor. 12:12). It says that one of the great names for Jesus is "Wonderful Counselor" (Isa. 9:6). It notes that we are "fearfully and wonderfully made" and that all God's "works are wonderful" (Ps. 139:14). The Psalms contain this idea especially. In the New International Version the words *wonder, wonderful,* and their derivatives occur thirty-two times in the Psalter.

The writer of Psalm 119 had not lost his sense of wonder, because he found the Bible to be wonderful. Early in the psalm he prays: "Open my eyes that I may see wonderful things in your law" (v. 18). Further along he speaks of meditating "on your wonders" (v. 27). Now in verse 129 he asserts, "Your statutes are wonderful; therefore I obey them." Wonder is the theme of the *pe* and *tsadhe* stanzas (vv. 129–44).

127

First there is the wonder of God's Law and then the obedience that follows from a proper appreciation of it. Wonder and obedience are linked throughout the stanzas, the word "obey" being repeated three times in verses 129, 134, and 136.

How wonderful is God's Word? Spurgeon writes a splendid paragraph about it. It is

> full of wonderful revelations, commands, and promises. Wonderful in their nature, as being free from all error, and bearing within themselves overwhelming self-evidence of their truth; wonderful in their effects as instructing, elevating, strengthening, and comforting the soul. Jesus the eternal Word is called Wonderful, and all the uttered words of God are wonderful in their degree. Those who know them best wonder at them most. It is wonderful that God should have borne testimony at all to sinful men, and more wonderful still that his testimony should be of such a character, so clear, so full, so gracious, so mighty.[2]

As to the psalmist's obedience: "Their [God's words] wonderful character so impressed itself upon his mind that he kept them in his memory; their wonderful excellence so charmed his heart that he kept them in his life."[3]

These two stanzas offer seven reasons why God's words are wonderful.

They Give Understanding

The psalmist says God's words are wonderful because they give "understanding to the simple." He states this in verse 130 and records his obedient response in verse 131.

> The unfolding of your words gives light;
>   it gives understanding to the simple.
> I open my mouth and pant,
>   longing for your commands.

"Unfolding" is an interesting term. The Hebrew word is *pethach*. But depending on the pronunciation, it can mean either "door" (with a short *e*) or "revelation" (with a long *e*). The New International Version, following the King James, takes it the first way, saying, "The unfolding of your words gives light." Martin Luther thought it had to do with revelation; so his translation read, *"Wenn dein Wort offenbar wird"* ("When your word is revealed"). The explanation for this double meaning is that in the early days of the formation of the Hebrew language the Jews were bedouins, who lived in tents. The only opening in a tent was the flap of skin that was the door. So when the door was unfolded light came into the tent, illuminating everything that was inside. The writer captures this exactly when he speaks of the "unfolding" of God's words giving light.

Haven't you found that to be true? Reading the Bible throws light on life, on all its problems and trials, on the confusing behavior of other people, on what is important and what is not, on right behavior, right goals, and right priorities. If you have not found this to be true, it is because of one of two things. Either you are not really studying the Bible or you are approaching it in a superior or vain frame of mind, judging it by your own limited views rather than allowing it to judge you. You need to allow the Bible to instruct you.

Martin Luther pointed out that the Word gives understanding "to the simple," which is what the verse says. He argued that the wisdom of the Bible is hidden from those who are wise in their own eyes but that it is disclosed to those who are "ready, prepared, eager always to be taught, judged, and to hear, rather than to teach, judge, and be heard."[4]

How this works is illustrated by the way Jesus dealt with the Emmaus disciples in the story recorded in Luke 24. These two people, probably Cleopas and his wife Mary, were returning home after the crucifixion when Jesus caught up to them on the road. They did not recognize him. When he asked why they were downcast, they replied by telling him what had happened in Jerusalem at the time of the Passover.

They told him about Jesus: "He was a prophet, powerful in word and deed before God and all the people" (Luke 24:19). They told him how the chief priests and rulers "handed him over to be sentenced to death, and . . . crucified him" (v. 20). As they related their experience it came out that they had been in Jerusalem that very morning and had heard tales from the women who had been to the tomb, reporting that the body was no longer there and that angels had appeared proclaiming that Jesus was alive. This had not interested them. They did not believe in resurrections. They had not even bothered to go to the tomb to see it for themselves, although they were within a short walk of the burial garden.

Jesus began to teach them from the Scriptures. "How foolish you are, and how slow of heart to believe all that the prophets have spoken! Did not the Christ have to suffer these things and then enter his glory?" Then beginning with Moses and going through all the prophets "he explained to them what was said in all the Scriptures concerning himself" (vv. 25–27).

This story and its sequel—when Jesus appears to the rest of the disciples—contain three great revelations called "openings," just like the word "unfolding" in our psalm. The first is the opening of the Scriptures. After Jesus had disappeared from their sight, these two disciples said to each other, "Were not our hearts burning within us while he talked with us on the road and *opened the Scriptures* to us?" (v. 32, italics mine). Second, "*their eyes were opened* and they recognized him" (v. 31, italics mine). The third of these "openings" is mentioned in verse 45: "Then *he opened their minds* so they could understand the Scriptures" (italics mine).

That is how we grow in a knowledge of God's truth. First, there is the opening of God's Word, then the opening of the eyes to see Jesus, and finally the opening of the mind or understanding.

Notice that here, as in each of the other points to be considered, the end result is not understanding alone, but obedience to what is understood. That is why verse 131 follows verse 130. Because the unfolding of God's words gives light, the poet says that he opens his mouth, panting after those words, longing for God's commands. The verse reminds me of Psalm 81:10 where God makes the promise: "Open wide your mouth and I will fill it."

We Find Mercy in These Pages

The second reason God's words are wonderful is that we find the mercy of God in them, and mercy is what we need—not justice, not pity, not recognition of tarnished "good" deeds, but a mercy that reaches out to save those who are truly wretched and helpless because of sin. The psalmist expresses this idea as a prayer: "Turn to me and have mercy on me, as you always do to those who love your name" (v. 132).

This verse is the last of the verses in Psalm 119 that do not mention the Word of God specifically, though it is possible that "your name" refers indirectly to the words of God. Whatever the case, it is in the Bible that the psalmist finds mercy, and the mercy of God to sinners is the most wonderful of all wonders. Charles Wesley captured it a bit in his greatest hymn, "And Can It Be," particularly in the third verse:

> He left his Father's throne above,
> So free, so infinite his grace;
> Emptied himself of all but love,
> And bled for Adam's helpless race;
> 'Tis mercy all, immense and free;
> For, O my God, it found out me.

Have you found the mercy of God in the Word of God? Until you have, you will never think of the Bible as being wonderful. You need to pray the prayer of the publican, the tax collector who stood at the edge of the crowd and cried, "God, have mercy on me, a sinner" (Luke 18:13). He found mercy through the shed blood of Jesus Christ and went home justified, according to Jesus. You will too if you allow the Bible to point you to Christ and if you put your faith in him, the Savior of sinners.

They Give Direction for Life

The third reason the psalmist finds the words of God wonderful is something we have noticed many times already. It is because they give right guidance for his life. They give direction for his footsteps, victory over sin, and salvation from those who have been trying to destroy him (vv. 133–34). This has been a recurring theme throughout the psalm. What is new in these verses is the emphasis on obedience. This emphasis is found throughout the *pe* stanza. It is by obeying God's Word that the writer finds direction, victory, and deliverance. Yet the reverse is also true. It is because he has found direction, victory, and deliverance from God's Word that he determines to obey it.

God Is in Them

The psalmist finds the Scriptures wonderful because God himself is in them and reveals himself to the one who studies them. "Make your face shine upon your servant," the writer says (v. 135). This verse is a conscious echo of the Old Testament benediction, known as the Aaronic blessing:

> The LORD bless you
>   and keep you;
> the LORD make his face shine upon you
>   and be gracious to you;
> the LORD turn his face toward you
>   and give you peace.
> Numbers 6:24–26

What was the great longing and aspiration of the Old Testament saints, the greatest blessing they could possibly conceive? It was to see the face of God. That is why Moses asked to see God in that poignant exchange found in Exodus 33. Moses wanted to see God face to face. God told him that he could not grant his request, because "no one may see me and live" (v. 20). Nevertheless, God placed Moses in a cleft of the mountains, covered him with his hand, and passed by saying, "The LORD, the LORD, the compassionate and gracious God, slow to anger, abounding in love and faithfulness, maintaining love to thousands, and forgiving wickedness, rebellion and sin" (Exod. 34:6–7). In that way Moses did indeed "see" him.

That is how we see God too, not in some imaginary, direct, unmediated revelation of God to souls, but in the Bible. It is there alone that we see God. Jesus told the disciples, "Anyone who has seen me has seen the Father" (John 14:9), but it is in the Bible that we see Jesus.

Verse 136 is the third of the verses in this stanza that contain the idea of obedience. But here the writer's concern is that God's law is "not obeyed." This brings tears to his eyes because of the dishonor it is to God and also because of the misery and harm it brings to those who are guilty of disobedience.

We need to learn from this today. Instead of weeping over people who disobey and even flaunt God's laws, many Christians in our time get angry with such persons and fight them verbally, and sometimes even physically. Matthew Henry said, "The sins of sinners are the sorrows of saints." Jesus wept over Jerusalem (Luke 19:41). Paul said that he had "great sorrow and unceasing anguish" in his heart because of the widespread unbelief of Israel (Rom. 9:1–4). Tears show compassion, and compassion wins others far more effectively than belligerent arguments and certainly more than anger. Do we weep for others, sorrowing over the pain we know their unbelief and disobedience bring?

They Are Altogether Righteous

The theme of the next stanza of Psalm 119 is righteousness, doubtless because the Hebrew word for "righteous" *(tsedek)* begins with the letter that starts each verse in this section *(tsadhe)* and was the obvious word with which to begin. But even more than that, it is close to the word for the letter both in spelling and pronunciation. "Righteousness" is found in verses 137, 138, 142, and 144.

This is another reason the psalmist found God's words wonderful. They are altogether righteous. Two thoughts go together in these references. First, the source of righteousness is the character of God ("Righteous are you, O LORD," v. 137; "Your righteousness is everlasting," v. 142). Second, the law of God gives expression to that righteousness ("your laws are right," v. 137; "The statutes you have laid down are righteous," v. 138; "Your statutes are forever right," v. 144). A way we might express this is to say that the Bible mirrors the character of God. This means that anyone who cares about righteousness and wants to act righteously should study the Bible. Statesmen should study it. So should judges, policemen, teachers, parents, ministers—indeed, everyone who believes that morality matters.

They Have Been Tested and Proved

In the middle of this discussion of the righteousness of God's laws a new, sixth reason why God's Word is wonderful occurs. It is that God's words have been tested and proved to be reliable (vv. 140–41). In other words, they really do give understanding; disclose God to be a God of great mercy; provide direction for life, victory over sin, and deliverance from man's oppression; reveal God himself; and teach what true righteousness is. Moreover, they show that God, who has given the Scriptures, can be trusted, since all his promises are "amen and amen." They never fail to be fulfilled.

Have you found God's word to be fully trustworthy? Years ago there were Christians who used to put the promises of God to the test and when they received what was promised would write "T and P" in their Bible next to the promise. The letters stood for "tried and proven," exactly what the psalmist says he found to be true in his experience.

They Are True

The last of these seven reasons the Word of God is wonderful in the view of the psalmist is because God's words are true. "Your law is true," he says (v. 142). This is important because much of what we hear from other sources, even those considered to be reputable and reliable, is false. Who trusts anyone's words today? A number of years ago two researchers, James Patterson and Peter Kim, wrote *The Day America Told the Truth* in which they claimed that Americans lie all the time and often for no apparent reason.[5] Politicians lie. Directors of large corporations lie. Employees lie. Husbands and wives lie.

Is there anyone who does not lie? God does not lie. God is truth itself. Every word he has ever spoken can be trusted. Every word! And that is truly wonderful!

12

Using God's Word in Prayer

I call with all my heart; answer me, O LORD,
    and I will obey your decrees.
I call out to you; save me
    and I will keep your statutes.
I rise before dawn and cry for help;
    I have put my hope in your word.
My eyes stay open through the watches of the night,
    that I may meditate on your promises.
Hear my voice in accordance with your love;
    preserve my life, O LORD, according to your laws.
Those who devise wicked schemes are near,
    but they are far from your law.
Yet you are near, O LORD,
    and all your commands are true.
Long ago I learned from your statutes
    that you established them to last forever.

Psalm 119:145–52

WE ARE NEARING THE END OF PSALM 119, SO IT IS NOT SUR-
prising that the danger that has threatened the psalmist all

along should emerge again strongly, though not for the final time. It has to do with his relentless enemies. The presence of these enemies has been alluded to earlier.[1] But verses 145–52 seem to concentrate on this reality: "I call out to you; save me" (v. 146); "I rise before dawn and cry for help" (v. 147); "Those who devise wicked schemes are near" (v. 150).

What is to be done in the face of their cruel threats and machinations? We know the answer. The writer turns to God in prayer, praying as though there were an open Bible before him. His Bible reminds him that although "those who devise wicked schemes are near" (v. 150), God is also "near" (v. 151). And that makes all the difference! Derek Kidner writes, "The threat is not glossed over; it is put in perspective by a bigger fact."[2]

Yet these verses are not really about the psalmist's enemies, as bad as they are. They are about the writer's prayer life and how he has learned to use God's Word in prayer. Charles Haddon Spurgeon suggested an eight-part outline for this section, one point for each of its eight verses: (1) how David prayed (v. 145); (2) what he prayed for (v. 146); (3) when he prayed (v. 147); (4) how long he prayed (v. 148); (5) what he pleaded (v. 149); (6) what happened (v. 150); (7) how he was rescued (v. 151); and (8) what was his witness to the whole matter (v. 152).[3] I will comment on the stanza by using a four-part outline, but Spurgeon's points alert us to how much can be learned about prayer from these verses.

Praying Earnestly

Prayer should be deeply earnest. The psalmist's prayers were, and it is this that drove him to God's Word. The fact that he was driven to the Bible again and again is expressed in almost every verse of this section. But his fervency in prayer emerges most clearly in the first two verses, which say that he is calling to God to answer him and save him, and that he is doing this "with all [his] heart."

In the Hebrew text, as well as in English, the petitions "answer me" and "save me" are short, staccato utterances, which are appropriate for one who is in trouble and earnestly seeking help. In different circumstances a person might pray more leisurely with carefully thought-out petitions. He might even compose a prayer. Most of the psalms are carefully composed petitions. But there is not time for that when one is in trouble! Then one prays earnestly, seriously, desperately. And even if one is not in trouble, earnestness in prayer is an important prayer element.

Here are two instructive examples from the New Testament.

Peter's Prayer

First, we think of Peter when he was sinking in the water on the Sea of Galilee. His prayer to Jesus was identical to that of the psalmist. Jesus had been teaching on the Gentile side of Galilee and when he had finished his teaching and had fed the crowds, he sent his disciples in a boat ahead of him to the other side of the lake while he remained behind to pray in the hills overlooking the lake. The boat ran into stormy weather, and while the disciples were working hard to bring it to safety, Jesus came to them walking on the water. They were afraid. They thought they were seeing a ghost. But when Jesus called out, "Take courage! It is I. Don't be afraid," Peter realized that it was Jesus and asked Jesus if he could come to him on the water.

"Come," Jesus said.

The story continues, "Then Peter got down out of the boat, walked on the water and came toward Jesus. But when he saw the wind, he was afraid and, beginning to sink, cried out, 'Lord, save me!'" (Matt. 14:29–30). And Jesus did! Jesus reached out his hand immediately, caught Peter, and brought him back to the boat and safety.

That is what we can do and what we can experience. When we cry to Jesus to save us, we find that he is not far away and that he is ready to answer us and save us immediately. It is when our prayers are most earnest and we are most desperate that we are most immediately heard.

Elijah's Prayer

James has a lot to say about prayer, and toward the end of his letter, he picks up on this important theme again saying that "the prayer of a righteous man is powerful and effective" (James 5:16). The New King James Version says, "The effective, fervent prayer of a righteous man avails much." Then James offers the example of Elijah. "Elijah was a man just like us. He prayed earnestly that it would not rain, and it did not rain on the land for three and a half years. Again he prayed, and the heavens gave rain, and the earth produced its crops" (James 5:17–18).

Elijah had the same weaknesses we have. After his victory on Mount Carmel when the fire of God consumed Jehovah's sacrifice and the prophets of Baal were all taken away and killed, Jezebel warned Elijah: "May the gods deal with me, be it ever so severely, if by this time tomorrow I do not make your life like that of one of them" (1 Kings 19:2). Elijah was terrified and hid. Obviously, he was sometimes weak and fearful. Nevertheless, says James, Elijah was a man who was used by God to speak spiritual words and bring judgment on Ahab's kingdom.

God told Elijah to tell the king that it would not rain, and it did not. The grass dried up; the crops withered; the animals began to die. The kingdom was devastated. Then, after three years, God sent Elijah to tell Ahab that it would rain again.

Elijah went up to Mount Carmel. He put his head between his knees in an attitude of prayer and sent a servant to the edge of the hill to look for some indication of rain. The boy returned saying that all he saw was a broad expanse of blue sky over the Mediterranean.

Elijah told him to go look again. The boy went back, and Elijah continued to pray earnestly. When the boy returned, Elijah asked again if he saw anything. Nothing. The sky was absolutely clear. Elijah sent the young man back seven times.

The seventh time the servant reported, "A cloud as small as a man's hand is rising from the sea." Elijah knew that was it. So he said, "Go and tell Ahab, 'Hitch up your chariot and go down before the rain stops you'" (1 Kings 18:44). Then Elijah gathered up his robes and ran ahead, outdistancing Ahab's chariot. The rains came down, and the drought was broken.

James is reminding us how God worked through Elijah when he prayed earnestly. And he is encouraging us to be people of earnest prayer too—not men and women of presumption, who get an idea in their heads and baptize it by prayer, saying, "This is what God is going to do," when God had promised nothing of the sort. God wants his people to earnestly seek his will and pray for it and thus become agents of the blessing God brings. At the end of the Book of James he even gives us a place to start, suggesting that we pray for sinners. For "whoever turns a sinner from the error of his way will save him from death and cover over a multitude of sins" (James 5:20).

Praying Always

Paul was accustomed, at the end of his letters, to giving some practical applications of his earlier teaching. In Paul's first letter to the Thessalonians, when he comes to the closing section, he tells these believers to "pray continually," that is, at all times (1 Thess. 5:17). The writer of Psalm 119 seems to have learned this lesson too, since the next pair of verses speak of his daily prayer pattern. He begins his prayers even before sunrise and continues even into the watches of the night.

I rise before dawn and cry for help;
    I have put my hope in your word.
My eyes stay open through the watches of the night,
    that I may meditate on your promises.

verses 147–48

When Paul told the Thessalonians to "pray continually," he did not mean that they were to do nothing but pray. If they were doing that they would never be able to get anything else done. He meant instead that prayer is to be a natural and consistent part of our lives. It is not to be restricted only to special prayer seasons or special prayer days. We are to be people whose lives are consistently marked by an attitude of prayer.

And yet, there is something to be said for specific prayer times, since these fix our minds on God's words and determine how we will be thinking and acting in the remaining hours. The psalmist seems to have prayed early in the morning—"before dawn"—and "through the watches of the night." In other words, he was a person committed to strong spiritual disciplines, and regular morning and evening prayer times, together with Bible study, were important parts of his discipline.

One very important word that we have not yet adequately considered in this study of Psalm 119 is *meditate*. It occurs in verse 148 as an explanation for why the writer remained awake during the watches of the night. It was "that I may meditate on your promises." Christians today very much need to learn about and develop the habit of biblical meditation.

Biblical meditation is more than merely reading the Bible and perhaps praying afterwards. It is even more than memorizing certain portions of the Bible. It is internalizing the Bible's teaching to such an extent that the truths discovered in the Bible become part of how we think and change the way we function. It is what God demanded of Joshua when he was about to lead the people of Israel in the conquest of Canaan:

Be strong and very courageous. Be careful to obey all the law
my servant Moses gave you; do not turn from it to the right or
to the left, that you may be successful wherever you go. Do not
let this Book of the Law depart from your mouth; *meditate on
it day and night,* so that you may be careful to do everything
written in it. Then you will be prosperous and successful.

Joshua 1:7–8, italics mine

One person who knows a great deal about biblical meditation is Ronald A. Jenson, former president of the School of
Theology of the International Christian Graduate University.
In a booklet published by the International Council of Biblical Inerrancy, he tells how he had developed a successful
pornography business when he was still in elementary school,
buying sexually explicit literature and pictures and selling them
to friends at a profit. He ran it out of his basement. When he
became a Christian, he changed dramatically. He abandoned
his pornography business, becoming active in church work.
But even though he was now a committed Christian, he still
had trouble with his thought life because the pornographic
material he had been feeding on had become part of who he
was. He described it by saying, "When you sow a thought, you
reap an action. When you sow that action, you reap a habit.
When you sow that habit, you reap a character. When you sow
that character, you reap a destiny."[4] He had been sowing lustful thoughts, and a lustful character had been formed.

What delivered him from a pornographic pattern of life
was discovering how to meditate on the Bible's teaching. He
learned how to be transformed "by the renewing of [his]
mind" (Rom. 12:2). Meditation involved thinking what the
passage he was studying was about and internalizing it, imag-
ining what it would mean for him in specific acts of conduct.
He even worked on singing specific verses to whatever tune
seemed to fit them, because singing helped fix the biblical
truths in his mind. He was changed. His conclusion was this:
"Biblical meditation is hard work, but the reward is worth
it—a consistent, victorious Christian life."[5]

Praying Biblically

The third thing the poet teaches about prayer in these verses is that prayer is best when it is biblical, that is, when it accompanies and flows from serious Bible study and when it is, in a sense, repeating God's very words, teachings, decrees, and promises back to him. That is when our own prayer words become biblical. The psalmist expresses this when he talks about God hearing him "in accordance with your love" and preserving his life "according to your laws" (v. 149). What distresses him about the wicked is that "they are far from your law" (v. 150).

In his homiletical commentary on Ephesians, Harry Ironside tells about meeting an older, very godly man early in his ministry. The man, Andrew Fraser, was dying of tuberculosis, and Ironside went to visit him. Fraser could barely speak above a whisper because his lungs were almost consumed by the disease. But he said, "Young man, you are trying to preach Christ, are you not?"

"Yes, I am," replied Ironside.

"Well," he said, "sit down a little, and let us talk together about the Word of God." He opened his Bible, and until his strength was gone he unfolded one passage after another, teaching truths that Ironside before that time had not appreciated or even perceived. Before long, tears were running down Ironside's cheeks and he asked, "Where did you get these things? Can you tell me where I can find a book that will open them up to me? Did you get them in a seminary or college?"

Fraser replied, "My dear young man, I learned these things on my knees on the mud floor of a little sod cottage in the north of Ireland. There with my open Bible before me, I used to kneel for hours at a time and ask the Spirit of God to reveal Christ to my soul and to open the Word to my heart. He taught me more on my knees on that mud floor than I ever could have learned in all the seminaries or colleges in the world."[6]

That is the secret. I am not disparaging education, of course. I have received a great deal of it myself and have profited from it. But it is possible to have a great deal of theological education and still know very little about God, if that learning is only intellectual or academic. What counts is time spent prayerfully in the Bible.

Praying in Faith

The fourth truth to be learned about prayer in these verses is that prayer must be in faith, believing. I referred earlier to the book of James because James has so much to say about prayer, especially at the close of chapter 5. But James also writes about prayer in chapter 1. In that chapter he is urging us to pray for wisdom, promising that if a man asks for wisdom, God will give it. Then he adds wisely,

> But when he asks, he must believe and not doubt, because he who doubts is like a wave of the sea, blown and tossed by the wind. That man should not think he will receive anything from the Lord; he is a double-minded man, unstable in all he does.
>
> James 1:6–8

But suppose we do doubt. And we do! What then? Clearly we must ask God even for the faith we need to pray in faith. We must be like the man who asked Jesus to heal his demon possessed son (Mark 9:22–24). He begged Jesus, "If you can do anything, take pity on us and help us."

"'If you can'?" said Jesus in mild surprise. "Everything is possible for him who believes."

The man exclaimed, "I do believe; help me overcome my unbelief!" And Jesus healed his son.

Like that desperate father, our faith is not strong. It is always mixed with unbelief and doubt and at the best it is still weak. But God gives faith and strengthens faith. Moreover, we do not need an overwhelming amount of faith for God to

145

hear us, since the believer's strength is not in his or her faith but in God, who is faith's object. We remember how Jesus also said, "If you have faith as small as a mustard seed, you can say to this mountain, 'Move from here to there' and it will move. Nothing will be impossible for you" (Matt. 17:20).

How is this faith cultivated? It is cultivated by studying the Bible and learning what God is like. As we study the Bible, we get to know God, and our faith is made strong because it is in him.

The psalmist did this. The stanza tells us that he studied the Bible prayerfully day and night and that what he learned specifically when he did study the Bible was that although his enemies were "near" (v. 150), God was also "near" (v. 151). This is the truth we saw at the beginning of this chapter. This tells us that it is the presence of God perceived in Bible study that frees us from our fears and makes us strong in faith. The last line says about God's statutes, "you established them to last forever." The person who builds on them will also stand firm and forever. We sing about it in the hymn I quoted from in chapter 7. Here are the second and last stanzas:

> Fear not, I am with thee, O be not dismayed;
> For I am thy God, I will still give thee aid;
> I'll strengthen thee, help thee, and cause thee to stand,
> Upheld by my gracious, omnipotent hand.

> The soul that on Jesus hath leaned for repose,
> I will not, I will not desert to his foes;
> That soul, though all hell should endeavor to shake,
> I'll never, no never, no never forsake.

Nothing is more certain than your security in Jesus Christ. Jesus was ordained to be your Savior from sin before the foundation of the world, which means that your salvation has been fixed from eternity in the eternal and unchangeable plan of God. Jesus achieved your salvation by his perfect atonement for the sins of his people in time. God has promised that nothing will ever separate from him those who are Christ's. We need to learn this not superficially or intellectually only, but firmly fixing it in our minds and living it with confidence. The only way that will ever happen—the only way God's people will ever be strong in faith, unshaken by enemies and by life's many trials—is by prayerful Bible study.

13

Obedience while Waiting

Look upon my suffering and deliver me,
   for I have not forgotten your law.
Defend my cause and redeem me;
   preserve my life according to your promise.
Salvation is far from the wicked,
   for they do not seek out your decrees.
Your compassion is great, O LORD;
   preserve my life according to your laws.
Many are the foes who persecute me,
   but I have not turned from your statutes.
I look on the faithless with loathing,
   for they do not obey your word.
See how I love your precepts;
   preserve my life, O LORD, according to your love.
All your words are true;
   all your righteous laws are eternal.

Rulers persecute me without cause,
   but my heart trembles at your word.
I rejoice in your promise
   like one who finds great spoil.
I hate and abhor falsehood
   but I love your law.

Seven times a day I praise you
    for your righteous laws.
Great peace have they who love your law,
    and nothing can make them stumble.
I wait for your salvation, O LORD,
    and I follow your commands.
I obey your statutes,
    for I love them greatly.
I obey your precepts and your statutes,
    for all my ways are known to you.

Psalm 119:153–68

THERE IS A LINK BETWEEN THE LAST STANZA (vv. 145–52) AND these two stanzas (vv. 153–68). The enemies of the psalmist are still present, as they have been throughout the psalm, and he is still praying: "Deliver me" (v. 153), "defend my cause and redeem me" (v. 154), "preserve my life" (vv. 154, 156, 159). Derek Kidner says that there even seems to be "a mounting urgency" in these repeated pleas for salvation.[1] At the same time there is also a significant change as we move from the former stanza to these two. The last set of verses was almost entirely a prayer. In these stanzas (stanzas twenty and twenty-one) the petitions tend to drop away—stanza twenty-one has no explicit prayers at all—and in their place comes a quiet, obedient waiting on God.

In other words, obedience is the new element. It is introduced in a negative way concerning the ungodly in verse 158 ("the faithless . . . do *not obey* your word"), and it reappears twice positively at the end (in verses 167 and 168, italics mine):

I *obey* your statutes,
    for I love them greatly.
I *obey* your precepts and your statutes,
    for all my ways are known to you.

This writer knows that obedience is not optional. He knows that it is essential to genuine discipleship and that it is the only basis on which he can have any claim on God for his swift intervention and deliverance.

Profession without Practice

But how little obedience there often is, even in strong Christian circles! I suppose that is why Jesus spoke about it so directly toward the end of the Sermon on the Mount (Luke's version). Jesus had been followed by many people who made a verbal profession of discipleship. They called him "Lord," which meant that they were calling him their master and were putting themselves forward as his servants. But they were also disregarding his teaching. Jesus showed the impossibility of this obvious contradiction by asking pointedly: "Why do you call me, 'Lord, Lord,' and do not do what I say?" (Luke 6:46). He was teaching that he is not our Lord if we do not obey him; and if he is not our Lord, then we do not even belong to him. We are like the man whose house was swept away by a flood (v. 49).

Disobedience, which is profession without practice, has been a problem throughout history. It was true of Israel. On the day before Ezekiel learned of the fall of the city of Jerusalem to the Babylonians, the Lord appeared to him to explain why this was happening, and the explanation was in terms of the people's lack of obedience.

God told Ezekiel,

Your countrymen are talking together about you by the walls and at the doors of the houses, saying to each other, "Come and hear the message that has come from the Lord." My people come to you, as they usually do, and sit before you to listen to your words, but they do not put them into practice. With their mouths they express devotion, but their hearts are greedy for unjust gain. Indeed, to them you are nothing more than one who sings love songs with a beautiful voice and plays an instrument well, for they hear your words but do not put them into practice.

Ezekiel 33:30–32

Jerusalem was destroyed because the people wanted only to be entertained by God's words, not to obey his instructions. Should we expect God to react any differently to our disobedience today?

Isaiah said the same thing in words Jesus later referred to when he was teaching his disciples: "The Lord says: 'These people come near to me with their mouth and honor me with their lips, but their hearts are far from me'" (Isa. 29:13). Jesus also used this text to reprove teachers of the law who made a profession of adhering to God's words when actually they were obeying only man-made regulations. He called them "hypocrites" and "blind guides" (Matt. 15:1–14; Mark 7:1–16).

Apparently, the problem of profession without practice was also present in the early Christian community, as proved by the epistle of James.

Do not merely listen to the word, and so deceive yourselves. Do what it says. Anyone who listens to the word but does not do what it says is like a man who looks at his face in a mirror and, after looking at himself, goes away and immediately forgets what he looks like. But the man who looks intently into the perfect law that gives freedom, and continues to do this, not forgetting what he has heard, but doing it—he will be blessed in what he does.

James 1:22–25

There is nothing so obvious as the truth that "faith" without obedience is worthless, even contemptible. Yet there are few things so common as this. One writer says, "Open sin, and avowed unbelief, no doubt slay their thousands. But profession without practice slays its tens of thousands."[2] He means that those who disobey God will be carried away by life's torrents.

What the Psalmist Knows

The psalmist was not making this mistake. He knew that if he was serious about his discipleship, he would have to immerse himself in the Bible. And he knew that if he did immerse himself in the Bible, he would have to obey it. We sometimes think of obedience as something we just have to grit our teeth and do. But the psalmist thought of it as a joyous, natural response to what he learned about God when he studied his Word.

What had he learned? These stanzas give four answers.

1. *God is merciful* (v. 156). Our translation of this verse says, "Your compassion is great." But the same Hebrew words might be equally well rendered, "Many are your mercies." Whatever the translation, the fact that God is rich in mercy is the most wonderful thing we can know about him. We have already seen that this is what God revealed to Moses when he placed him in a cleft of mountain rock, covered him with his hand and passed by, saying, "The LORD, the LORD, the compassionate and gracious God, slow to anger, abounding in love and faithfulness, maintaining love to thousands, and forgiving wickedness, rebellion and sin" (Exod. 34:6–7). In the Old Testament, these two verses about God's mercy are more frequently echoed than any other Old Testament verse (Numbers 14:18; Deuteronomy 5:9–10; Nehemiah 9:17; Psalm 86:15; 103:8; 145:8; Joel 2:13; and Jonah 4:2). Mercy is what we all desperately need. As New Testament believers, we know that we have this mercy through the Lord Jesus Christ.

2. *God's word is true* (v. 160). This is a great lesson for the psalmist to have learned, or for anyone to learn. So it is not surprising that it figures strongly in these last stanzas. We find it in verse 142 ("your law is true"), verse 151 ("all your commands are true"), and verse 160 ("all your words are true").

Have you learned that about the Bible? Have you learned how true, how utterly trustworthy God's Word is, even when everything and everyone about you proves false and is untrustworthy? Spurgeon wrote,

The ungodly are false, but God's word is true. . . . God's word has been true from the first moment in which it was spoken, true throughout the whole of history, true to us from the instant in which we believed it, true to us before we were true to it. . . . The Scriptures are as true in Genesis as in Revelation, and the five books of Moses are as inspired as the four Gospels. Neither in the book of revelation nor of providence will there be any need to put a single note of *errata*. The Lord has nothing to regret or to retract, nothing to amend or to reverse.[3]

The Bible was as true for your grandmother and grandfather as it is for you. The same Word that speaks truthfully to you spoke truthfully to poor tillers of the soil in England two hundred years ago and to martyrs standing against the cruel persecutions of imperial Rome or the church's own terrible inquisition in the Middle Ages. If you turn from the Word of God, you do not turn to something more truthful. You turn to lies.

3. *Personal peace comes from personal obedience* (v. 165). The third thing the poet learned from his study of the Bible is that peace is the reward of those who obey God's law. In the Hebrew of this verse "peace" is the word *shalom*. Like the word *salvation* to which it is closely linked, *shalom* is a large, embracing word for all the good that comes to the one God favors.[4] It has to do with personal well-being in all respects. On the spiritual level it embraces "peace with God" through the work of Jesus Christ. On the material level it can mean prosperity, even an abundance of riches. On the personal level it has to do with a tranquil state of mind that comes from placing one's entire hope in God's Word. Alexander Maclaren preached a sermon in which he spoke of this personal peace as encompassing "a restful heart, . . . a submitted will, . . . an obedient life . . . [and] freedom from temptations."[5]

We should note, however, that the verse does not promise peace only to those who perfectly keep God's law, for who can keep it? It promises peace to those who "love" God's law, which means, I suppose, those who love it because, by reading it, they have found God to be merciful. "We love [him] because he first loved us" (1 John 4:19).

4. *The obedient are secure* (v. 165). The fourth thing the psalmist says he learned by reading the Bible is that those who obey God's Word are secure. "Nothing can make them stumble." Where else can we find security in this life? Nowhere else, of course. Our only true security is in God.

I think here of a wonderful section of Saint Augustine's *City of God* in which that great father of the church reflects on the uncertainties of this life.

> What numberless casualties threaten our bodies . . . extremes of heat and cold, storms, floods, inundations, lightning, thunder, hail, earthquakes, houses falling; or from the stumbling, or shying, or vice of horses; from countless poisons in fruits, water, air, animals; from the painful or even deadly bites of wild animals; from the madness which a mad dog communicates, so that even the animal which of all others is most gentle and friendly to its own master, becomes an object of intenser fear than a lion or dragon, and the man whom it has by chance infected with this pestilential contagion becomes so rabid, that his parents, wife, children dread him more than any wild beast!
>
> What disasters are suffered by those who travel by land or sea! What man can go out of his own house without being exposed on all hands to unforeseen accidents? Returning home sound in limb, he slips on his own doorstep, breaks his leg, and never recovers. What can seem safer than a man sitting in his chair? Eli the priest fell from his, and broke his neck.[6]

Surely there is no security for any of us in this life except in loving and living by the unshakable and eternal Word of God.

Obedience and the Word of God

If trusting God involves obeying God's Word, as it certainly does, then there can be no real discipleship apart from

Bible study. Indeed, study of the Bible cannot even be an occasional, minor, or "vacation-time" pursuit. It must be the consuming passion of a believer's life. This is because it is only by the study of the Word of God that we learn what it is to obey God and follow Jesus. If you want to know God as he speaks to you through the Bible, you should study the Bible daily, systematically, comprehensively, devotionally, and prayerfully.

Daily Study

We can study the Bible more than once each day, of course. The psalmist has already spoken of rising early for his devotional time and of meditating on God's Word through the watches of the night. In the *shin* stanza (v. 164) he speaks of praising God "seven times a day," presumably in the context of serious Bible study.[7] But when he says that, the writer probably means only that he worshiped God continuously. What is important is that we discipline our lives to include regular periods of Bible study, just as we discipline ourselves to have regular periods for sleep, mealtimes, and so on. In fact the comparison with regular meals is a good one, for these are necessary if the body is to be healthy and if good work is to be done. On occasion we may miss a meal—missing a meal is not deadly—but normally we should not. In the same way, we must feed regularly on God's Word if we are to become strong in faith and remain strong spiritually.

What happens if we neglect regular Bible reading? We grow indifferent to God and lax in spiritual things. We throw ourselves open to temptation and the sin that easily follows.

Systematic Study

Some people read the Bible at random, dipping in here or there. This may be characteristic of the way they do most things in life, but it is a mistake in Bible study. It leads to a lack of spiritual depth that is often characteristic of American Christians. A far better system of Bible reading is a regular, disciplined study of certain books of the Bible as a whole. The psalmist did this. The proof is the great variety of terms he uses for the Scriptures, for he tells us that he was fully acquainted with its laws, promises, decrees, and other portions. As he saw it, the Bible embraces the law, statutes, ways, precepts, decrees, commands, words, and promises of God. He did not want to neglect even one of them.

Comprehensive Study

Along with the study of one book or section of the Bible, there should be an attempt to become acquainted with the Bible as a whole. This means reading it comprehensively. True, many parts of the Bible will not appeal to you at first. This is natural. But if you never make an attempt to become acquainted with them, you limit your growth and may even warp your understanding. Paul told Timothy. "*All* Scripture is God-breathed and is useful for teaching, rebuking, correcting and training in righteousness" (2 Tim. 3:16, italics mine). Jesus speaks throughout the Bible, not only in the red-ink portions (indicating Jesus' own words), but everywhere.

Devotional Study

Nothing is clearer in this psalm than the close, indissoluble link between knowledge of God and study of the Word of God, between loving God and loving the Bible.

There is a danger when we speak of daily, systematic, and comprehensive study of the Bible that we encourage a person to think that such study is therefore mechanical and can be pursued in much the same manner as one would study a secular text in a university. That is not the case. In other books we study to become wise. In reading the Bible we study to know God, hear his voice, and be changed by him as we grow in holiness.

And there is this too: If we really want the Bible to become a part of us so that, by this means, the mind of Christ becomes our mind, at least in part, then we must memorize important sections of Scripture. Our educational system does little to stress memorization today. Those who were educated a generation ago will testify, however, that what they memorized then, whether simple verses or more complex passages from Shakespeare or another distinguished writer, has remained with them and has become a part of who they are. That is what we need as Christians. We need to allow the Word of God to become a part of us. To have that happen, we must memorize it.

Pat Williams, the general manager of the Orlando Magic, is a very busy man. He is always under pressure. Nevertheless, he spends twenty minutes a day in uninterrupted Bible study and then spends whatever time is necessary each day to memorize one verse of the Bible. He has memorized a verse a day for years, and he testifies that this is the single most important factor in his spiritual growth.

Prayerful Study

It is impossible to study the Bible devotionally without praying. Prayer comes naturally to those engaged in Bible study. But although prayer is part of a devotional study of Scripture, prayer is worth stressing for its own sake, if only because we so often neglect it. The best way to study the Bible is to encompass the study in prayer. That is what we looked at in the last chapter.

Before we begin our Bible study, we should say, "Lord, God, I am turning to your Word. I cannot understand it as I should. I need your Holy Spirit to instruct me and draw a proper response from me. What I understand I want to obey. Help me to do that for Jesus' sake." Then we must study the passage and when we find something that pertains to our lives, we must stop and acknowledge that prayerfully. Without regular, personal Bible study and prayer, we are not really walking with Christ as his followers and we are certainly not obeying him in specific areas.

Deliverance from Sin and Self

Suppose we do pursue regular, personal Bible study. Suppose we do earnestly seek to know the mind of our Savior and obediently follow where he leads. What do we find then? Some would say that we plunge into a dull monotony of life or at best have a list of dull rules to follow. But those who actually follow Christ find something different. They find adventure in a life lived with God and a strong deliverance from self that is an amazing form of liberty.

Jesus taught this in his day. He had been expounding on the source of his teachings, and many who listened had believed on him. He told them, "If you hold to my teaching, you are really my disciples. Then you will know the truth, and the truth will set you free" (John 8:31–32). This angered some of his listeners. They replied, "We are Abraham's descendants and have never been slaves of anyone. How can you say that we shall be set free?" (v. 33). Jesus did not reply that they had actually been slaves to many foreign governments, though he could have. Instead, he spoke of bondage to sin and showed that true freedom consists in deliverance from sin through obedience. "I tell you the truth, everyone who sins is a slave to sin. . . . If the Son sets you free, you will be free indeed" (vv. 34, 36).

So it is! Obedience is not bondage. It is freedom. It comes as we determine to obey Jesus.

14

This Poor Sheep

May my cry come before you, O LORD;
  give me understanding according to your word.
May my supplication come before you;
  deliver me according to your promise.
May my lips overflow with praise,
  for you teach me your decrees.
May my tongue sing of your word,
  for all your commands are righteous.
May your hand be ready to help me,
  for I have chosen your precepts.
I long for your salvation, O LORD,
  and your law is my delight.
Let me live that I may praise you,
  and may your laws sustain me.
I have strayed like a lost sheep.
  Seek your servant,
  for I have not forgotten your commands.
Psalm 119:169–76

THERE IS A TREMENDOUS DIFFERENCE BETWEEN THIS STANZA and the preceding one. In fact there is a tremendous difference between this stanza and all the other stanzas of the psalm. The preceding stanza was all confident assertion: "I rejoice in your promise" (v. 162), "I hate and abhor falsehood" (v. 163); "I wait for your salvation" (v. 166); "I obey your precepts and your statutes" (v. 168). In this stanza all is petition, and there is little confidence at all. Instead, there is humble recognition of the writer's lost condition and his constant need of God's grace. "I have strayed like a lost sheep. Seek your servant, for I have not forgotten your commands" (v. 176).

This tells us that the author has not become self-righteous by his study, despite his repeated claims to have obeyed the Bible's teachings. This is what Derek Kidner saw in these verses, observing that "the love of Scripture . . . need not harden into academic pride. This man would have taken his stance not with the self-congratulating Pharisee of the parable, but with the publican who stood afar off but went home justified."[1]

Verse 175, the next to the last verse of the psalm, is a good biblical statement of what the Westminster Shorter Catechism calls "the chief end of man," namely, to glorify God and enjoy him forever: "Let me live that I may praise you." But verse 176, the last verse, reminds us that this praise comes from poor, weak, lost, and straying sinners like ourselves.

Simul Justus et Peccator

I have to take issue with some of the writers on this psalm, who argue that the psalmist cannot be thinking of himself as a lost sheep, in the same sense that the sheep in Jesus' parable is lost, since the psalmist is "one who does not forget God's commands."[2] They think that the issues here are not spiritual, that the psalmist is not writing about sin and salvation. They argue that he is thinking of himself as a lost sheep only in the sense of being exposed to enemies and thus being always in need of God's care.

But if that is the case, why does he speak of himself as having "strayed," rather than as merely being weak? Why does he ask God to "seek" him, rather than to strengthen or protect him? This is not the language of mere temporal distress. It is spiritual language, the language of Isaiah who wrote in his great fifty-third chapter, "We all, like sheep, have gone astray, each of us has turned to his own way" (v. 6).

What the writer of Psalm 119 is saying is that this is the only right description of himself as he is apart from the grace of God. He is a poor, lost sheep. So what is needed—what he needs and what we need too—is what Isaiah wrote about in the second half of the verse I just quoted. The poet needs that One on whom "the Lord has laid . . . the iniquity of us all."

What we have here is an example of what Martin Luther meant when he spoke of a believer in Christ being *simul justus et peccator*, that is, of being at once "both justified and a sinner." Luther wrote of verse 176, "This verse is extremely emotional and full of tears, for truly we are all thus going astray, so that we must pray to be visited, sought, and carried over by the most godly Shepherd, the Lord Jesus Christ, who is God blessed forever. Amen."[3]

Luther began his Ninety-five Theses, which he posted on the door of the Castle Church in Wittenberg at the commencement of the Protestant Reformation, with, "When our Lord and Master, Jesus Christ, said 'repent,' he meant that the entire life of believers should be one of repentance." In other words, there is never a moment, even after we are saved, when we can stop thinking of ourselves as lost sheep. Therefore, as another writer says, "The highest flights of human devotion must end in confession of sin. . . . The sincerest professions of human fidelity must give place to the acknowledgment of helplessness. . . . The loftiest human declarations of love to God's law must come down to the mournful acknowledgment that we have only not forgotten it."[4]

In this last verse, then, the psalmist is speaking of himself as he really is. Because of this, it might have been good to have studied this verse first, followed by the others. As it is, it might be useful even now to go back and study Psalm 119 all over again with these last prayers and this most humble self-description in mind.

The Psalmist's Sad Condition

In Psalm 23, the shepherd's psalm, David wrote of the many things he did not lack with God as his good shepherd. "I shall not be in want," he declares at the beginning (v. 1). And then he spells out God's gracious provision for him in detail, saying in essence, I shall not lack rest; I shall not lack life; I shall not lack guidance; I shall not lack safety; I shall not lack comfort; I shall not lack provision; I shall not lack heaven.[5] In the last verses of Psalm 119, by a helpful contrast, the writer lists what he *does* lack, unless God is his shepherd. He is lacking in five areas.

Lacking Understanding

The person who wrote this psalm was obviously blessed and inspired by the Holy Spirit. We might think that he would be conscious of how much he knows of God and God's ways, or at least of how much he is learning. But this is not how the psalmist is thinking. Instead of being aware of how much he knows, he is conscious of how little he knows and that if he is to understand anything at all about God and God's ways, God must open his eyes and give him understanding as he studies the Bible. So, as he begins this final stanza, he asks God for understanding. "May my cry come before you, O LORD; give me understanding according to your word" (v. 169).

If we think we are wise, we are the most foolish of all people. On the other hand, if we recognize our foolishness and come to God for his instruction, we can begin to gain wisdom. That is what Paul wrote to the Christians at Corinth who thought they were wise but who were allowing their pseudo wisdom and prejudices to divide the church.

Where is the wise man? Where is the scholar? Where is the philosopher of this age? Has not God made foolish the wisdom of the world? For since in the wisdom of God the world through its wisdom did not know him, God was pleased through the foolishness of what was preached to save those who believe. Jews demand miraculous signs and Greeks look for wisdom, but we preach Christ crucified: a stumbling block to Jews and foolishness to Gentiles, but to those whom God has called, both Jews and Greeks, Christ the power of God and the wisdom of God. For the foolishness of God is wiser than man's wisdom, and the weakness of God is stronger than man's strength.

1 Corinthians 1:20–25

The psalmist was writing before the birth of Jesus, of course. He did not know what we know about the life, death, and resurrection of Jesus, or even a whole lot about the gospel, though he probably looked for a Redeemer, the Messiah, to come. Nevertheless, he knew that all genuine understanding comes from God and that he needed to ask God for it. And so he does.

Needing Deliverance

The second thing the psalmist knew he lacked and therefore asks God to give him is deliverance: "Deliver me according to your promise" (v. 170). The word *deliverance* is a large word with many meanings, just like *salvation,* which is a close equivalent and even a possible translation of the Hebrew word in this sentence. *Deliverance* could mean deliverance from the power of death or enemies, which is how it has frequently been used in this psalm. Commentators who think that the poet is referring to himself as a lost sheep only in the sense of being weak and in danger from those who hate him interpret it this way. They think that when he says "deliver me," he must mean "deliver me from my enemies."

Perhaps this is correct, but if he is thinking of spiritual things, as I believe he is, then *deliver* does really mean what we refer to by the word *salvation*. It means deliverance from sin—from its penalty, power, and presence—from the evil influences and outlook of the world, and perhaps even from the power of the devil. Whatever the case, it is clear that in ourselves we are lacking the needed salvation. We can do nothing to deliver ourselves. So we need to ask God for salvation, which is what the psalmist does.

Charles Bridges believed the psalmist was thinking of deliverance in this sense, particularly because he speaks of it explicitly in verse 174: "I long for your salvation." This is the way Bridges wrote about it toward the end of his five-hundred-page commentary on this psalm. Bridges looked at the "fullness" of our salvation, which includes all the mercy of God's great covenant of grace. He looked at the "ground" of this salvation, the work of Christ on the cross. He looked too at the "simplicity" of salvation, not keeping the sinner away from God in useless moral striving or bewilderment, but opening the way through faith in Christ's atonement. He looked at the "unchangeableness" of our salvation, which is above and beyond and superior to all our weak feelings and failures. He concluded, "Is not this an object for the longing of the soul, that feels its own pressing wants and sees in this salvation an instant and full supply?"[6]

Is that your longing? Are you looking to God for the salvation that only he can supply? If you are not, it can only be because you do not have a true sense of need. You think you can handle things yourself. Learn from this psalm. These first petitions reflect the two great needs of fallen men and women, namely, to know God and to be saved from sin.

Right Worship

The psalmist is a saved man. Study of the Bible has taught him something of God and God's ways. He is trusting God to save him. But knowledge of God and salvation are not all he needs. If God is his Savior, he ought also to praise God for his salvation. How is he to do that? How are any of us to do it? If he is to worship God rightly, he needs two things. He needs to know what pleases God in worship, that is, the elements of worship that God has himself determined. And he needs to have a heart so filled with love for God that his worship is genuine and not merely the repetition of empty words or the practice of vain exercises. So he prays,

> May my lips overflow with praise,
>   for you teach me your decrees.
> May my tongue sing of your word,
>   for all your commands are righteous.
>
> verses 171–72

It comes as a surprise to many people to learn that God has fixed the ways by which we should worship him and that not all that passes for worship is acceptable. That was obvious in the Old Testament period. God was to be worshiped at the tabernacle (later the temple), and he was to be worshiped according to the Levitical priestly system. In fact, if people tried to approach him in any way other than by what he had determined, God's judgment was swift and terrible. We have examples in Nadab and Abihu, who offered unauthorized fire and were consumed (Lev. 10:1–2); Korah, who abrogated priestly functions to himself and was swallowed by the earth (Num. 16:1–35); or Uzziah, who offered incense, which only the priests could offer, and was judged by leprosy (2 Chron. 26:16–21).

God has prescribed acceptable forms of worship for people in the New Testament age too. We no longer worship in Jerusalem at the temple. It has been destroyed, and Jesus said, "God is spirit, and his worshipers must worship in spirit and in truth" (John 4:24). But that does not mean that just anything goes. "In truth" must mean according to the revelation of God in the Bible.

167

What does the Bible teach about how we should worship God today? Bible students differ about some elements: for example, whether it is right for ministers to wear clerical vestments, whether drama or liturgical dance are permitted, whether organs or other musical instruments can be used. There are churches, like Spurgeon's church in London, that permit only a cappella singing. And yet some things are quite clear. We are not to offer animal sacrifices, since Jesus' sacrifice of himself fulfilled the Old Testament requirement and abolished it forever. We are not to be raucous or immoral, as some had been in Corinth (see 1 Corinthians 11 and 14). Paul told the Corinthians, "Everything should be done in a fitting and orderly way" (1 Cor. 14:40). On the positive side, we are instructed to pray, sing hymns, and profit from the teaching of the Bible—especially concentrating on the Bible.

When the Protestant Reformation took place in the sixteenth century and the principles of the Word of God, which had long been covered over by the ceremonies of the medieval church, again became prominent, there was an immediate elevation of the Word of God in Protestant services. John Calvin particularly carried this out with thoroughness, ordering that the altars (long the center of the Latin mass) be removed from the churches and that a pulpit with a Bible on it be placed in the center of the building. This was not to be on one side of the room, but at the center, where every line of the architecture would carry the gaze of the worshiper to that Book.

This elevation of the Bible to a position of central importance was a good thing, something we do not want to lose today, though it is being lost in many churches. But how can we keep on track in such areas? And how do we develop a sincere, devout, and worshipful heart? The point of this is that we cannot do either by ourselves. We lack what we need to worship God. Therefore we need to do as the psalmist did and ask God for instruction about how to worship him and for the ability to follow that instruction.

Living Uprightly

The next two verses might be seen as asking God's help in dealing with enemies. But if the writer is thinking along spiritual lines, as I have been suggesting, then when he prays, "May your hand be ready to help me" (v. 173), what he is probably thinking of is power to obey the precepts and law of God, which he, in fact, mentions next (vv. 173–74).

How are we going to live an upright life? Certainly not by our own power or determination. The apostle Paul knew the futility of that, which is why he wrote, "I am unspiritual, sold as a slave to sin. . . . For what I want to do I do not do, but what I hate I do. . . . I know that nothing good lives in me, that is, in my sinful nature. . . . What a wretched man I am! Who will rescue me from this body of death?" (Rom. 7:14, 15, 18, 24). Fortunately, Paul knew the answer to his own question. Do we? The answer is: "Thanks be to God—through Jesus Christ our Lord!" (v. 25). Clearly, if we believed that we are unable to live for God by ourselves and yet really want to do it, we will come to God for help, as Paul does. We will pray, Lord, help me to live an upright life.

Strength to Persevere

Once we have learned to depend on God to help us live an upright life, we will keep on praying, for we will want to do it not just for the present moment, but to our life's end. We will pray as the psalmist, "Let me live that I may praise you, and may your laws sustain me" (v. 175).

Salvation Is of the Lord

We have been looking at what the psalmist means when he ends this great psalm by calling himself a lost sheep. In a sense, he has been anticipating the teaching of Jesus, who said, "Apart from me you can do nothing" (John 15:5). Nothing does not mean a little something. It means nothing, nothing at all. Yet all is not hopeless since, although in ourselves we can do nothing, it is also true, as Paul said, that "I can do everything through him who gives me strength" (Phil. 4:13).

I think the psalmist is telling us this as he gets to the very end. He remains God's "servant" (v. 176) even though he has described himself as lost (a lost sheep), and even though he has confessed his need for understanding, deliverance, right worship, an upright way of life, and perseverance, and even though he needs God to seek him since he will never find the way to God himself. He is poor, lost, weak, sinful, yes, even an unworthy servant (Luke 17:10), but still a servant of God. Although he has not been able to keep God's commandments, he has not forgotten them and knows that he will yet keep them—by the grace and power of his Master.

What a great blessing! And what a blessing for us if we, like the psalmist, are also God's servants! Charles Bridges wrote, "I cannot forbear to plead, that although a rebellious prodigal, I am still thy servant, thy child. I still bear the child's mark of an interest in thy covenant. . . . Let me then lie humbled and self-abased. But let me not forget my claim—what he has done for me."[7]

The meaning of these last two verses has been captured in a stanza by Richard Mant, an author cited by Charles Spurgeon in *The Treasury of David*.

> Though like a sheep estranged I stray,
> Yet have I not renounced thy way.
> Thine hand extend; thine own reclaim;
> Grant me to live, and praise thy name.[8]

When Jonah was praying from inside the great fish he summarized what he had learned of God by saying, "Salvation comes from the LORD" (Jonah 2:9). That was an important lesson, and it is the last important teaching of this psalm. What does the shepherd do with such weak, sinful, and helpless people as ourselves? Jesus said that when the sheep are lost, the shepherd hunts until he finds them (Luke 15:3–7). Indeed, he said of his own mission, "The Son of Man came to seek and to save what was lost" (Luke 19:10).

Notes

Chapter 1 First Things First

1. Derek Kidner, *Psalms 73–150: A Commentary on Books III–V of the Psalms* (Downers Grove, Ill.: InterVarsity Press, 1975), 416.

2. This George Wishart is not to be confused with the Scottish reformer and martyr by the same name who lived a century earlier and was executed at Saint Andrews in 1546.

3. Charles Haddon Spurgeon, *The Treasury of David: Psalms 88–119*, vol. 3a (Grand Rapids: Zondervan, 1966), 133.

4. The others are Psalms 9–10 (together), 25, 34, 37, 111, 112, and 145, nine in all. Not all of these are perfect alphabetical poems, however. In some, letters are missing; in others, the order of the letters is not exact. Proverbs 31:10–31 and the first four chapters of Lamentations also follow an acrostic pattern.

5. The story is in Rowland E. Prothero, *The Psalms in Human Life* (New York: E. P. Dutton, 1904), 327; and Spurgeon, *The Treasury of David*, 132.

6. Prothero, *The Psalms in Human Life*, 307; and Spurgeon, *The Treasury of David*, 133.

7. H. C. Leupold, *Exposition of the Psalms* (Grand Rapids: Baker, 1969), 824.

8. J. I. Packer, *Keep in Step with the Spirit* (Grand Rapids: Revell, 1984), 258–61.

Chapter 2 Starting Young

1. Herbert Lockyer Sr., *Psalms: A Devotional Commentary* (Grand Rapids: Kregel, 1993), 542. It would be farfetched to argue that each letter gives a theme to its particular stanza. However, *aleph*, the theme letter of verses 1–8, means "ox" in Hebrew, a useful beast of burden and hence a blessing to those who possess one, and blessing is the theme of that stanza: "Blessed are they whose ways are blameless" (v. 1).

2. This is not the only place in the psalm where the young are mentioned. The psalmist speaks as a young man again in verses 99 and 100, though without the use of that specific word. Does this mean that the writer of the psalm was himself a young man? Franz Delitzsch argued that he was, but this is not demanded by the language of the psalm. There is a good discussion of whether the psalmist is young or old in J. J. Stewart Perowne, who thinks the writer was neither young nor old but rather in middle life. See J. J. Stewart Perowne, *Commentary on the Psalms*, 2 vols. in 1 (1878–79; reprint, Grand Rapids: Kregel, 1989), 349–50; and Franz Delitzsch, *Biblical Commentary on the Psalms*, trans. Francis Bolton, vol. 3 (Grand Rapids: Eerdmans, n.d.), 243.

3. James Montgomery Boice, *Daniel: An Expositional Commentary* (Grand Rapids: Zondervan, 1989), 23–24.

4. Charles Bridges, *Psalm 119: An Exposition* (1827; reprint, Carlisle, Pa.: Banner of Truth Trust, 1977), 19.

173

Notes

5. Alexander Maclaren, *Expositions of Holy Scripture: The Psalms, Isaiah 1–48*, vol. 3 (Grand Rapids: Eerdmans, 1959), 286.

6. Spurgeon, *The Treasury of David*, 159. Herbert Lockyer has a similar outline: "The Best Possession—'Thy Word'/The Best Plan—'Have I hid'/The Best Place—'In my heart'/The Best Purpose—'That I might not sin against thee'" (Lockyer, *Psalms*, 544).

7. Martin Luther, *Luther's Works: First Lectures on the Psalms, Psalms 76–126*, ed. Hilton C. Oswald, vol. 2 (St. Louis: Concordia, 1976), 420.

Chapter 3 Trials on the Way

1. E. M. Blaiklock, *The Bible & I* (Minneapolis: Bethany, 1983).

2. Ibid., 91.

3. Saint Augustine, "The Confessions of St. Augustine" in *A Select Library of the Nicene and Post-Nicene Fathers of the Christian Church*, ed. Philip Schaff, vol. 1 (Grand Rapids: Eerdmans, 1974), 45.

4. Alexander Maclaren, *The Psalms: Psalms 90–150*, vol. 3 (New York: A. C. Armstrong and Son, 1894), 251.

5. Spurgeon, *The Treasury of David*, 177–78.

Chapter 4 In God's School

1. Leslie C. Allen, *Word Biblical Commentary: Psalms 101–150*, vol. 21 (Waco: Word, 1983), 142.

2. Bridges, *Psalm 119*, 84.

3. John R. W. Stott, *Your Mind Matters: The Place of the Mind in the Christian Life* (Downers Grove, Ill: InterVarsity Press, 1972).

4. See James Montgomery Boice, *Romans: The Reign of Grace, Romans 5–8*, vol. 2 (Grand Rapids: Baker, 1992), 649–56.

5. Stott, *Your Mind Matters*, 26.

6. Thomas Manton, *Psalm 119*, vol. 1 (1680; reprint, Carlisle, Pa.: The Banner of Truth Trust, 1990), 334.

7. Lockyer, *Psalms*, 549.

8. John Bunyan, *Pilgrim's Progress* (Norwalk, Conn.: The Easton Press, 1993), 95.

9. The four points in this section are from Spurgeon (from Marchant, one of the tutors at the Pastors' College), but I have handled them somewhat differently, basing them on verses 34–37, rather than verses 33–36 as Marchant did. This changes the order of the points. See Spurgeon, *The Treasury of David*, 213.

10. Delitzsch, *Biblical Commentary on the Psalms*, 249.

11. Maclaren, *The Psalms*, 256.

12. Leupold, *Exposition of the Psalms*, 831.

13. Manton, *Psalm 119*, 380–81. He works this out at length on pages 380–92.

Chapter 5 Finding God in His Word

1. Bruce Waltke, *Finding the Will of God: A Pagan Notion?* (Gresham, Ore.: Vision House, 1995), 89.

2. J. H. Merle D'Aubigné, *The Life and Times of Martin Luther*, trans. H. White (Chicago: Moody, 1958), 423–34.

3. Psalm 119:46 also appears at the head of the Augsburg Confession, in Latin from the Vulgate version: *Et loquebar de testimoniis tuis in conspectu regum et non confundebar.* Its choice as a theme verse for this confession of the German-speaking church reflects the Reformation experience.

4. This was an easy stanza for the psalmist to write because it is the *waw* stanza and *waw* means "and." Not many Hebrew words begin with *waw*, so the author has solved the problem by beginning each verse with "and." It reminds us of how "and" is sometimes used in English poetry to give a soft first syllable to lines, as in Wesley's hymn, beginning "And can it be that I should gain." Alexander Maclaren gives a translation of this stanza in which he was able to make each verse begin with "and":

> And let thy loving kindnesses come
>   to me, Jehovah . . .
> And I shall have a word to answer
>   him that reproaches me . . .

and so on. See Maclaren, *The Psalms*, 256.

Notes

5. Spurgeon, *The Treasury of David*, 254.

6. The account of the distribution of the priestly cities to Levi is in Joshua 21.

7. Lockyer, *Psalms*, 558.

8. Leupold, *Exposition of the Psalms*, 836.

Chapter 6 Affliction

1. This is the way C. S. Lewis states the critic's objection at the start of his study of human suffering in *The Problem of Pain* (New York: Macmillan, 1962), 26. It is also the problem raised by the Boston rabbi Harold S. Kushner in *When Bad Things Happen to Good People* (New York: Avon, 1981), though Kushner, being a rabbi, does not deny God's existence. He solves the problem by denying God's omnipotence. He advises us to love God and "forgive him despite his limitations" (p. 148).

2. Lockyer, *Psalms*, 565.

3. This is the ultimate meaning of history, which embraces the meaning of suffering, in my judgment. I discuss this concept at greater length in the last chapter, "Check It Out," of my book *Mind Renewal in a Mindless Age* (Grand Rapids: Baker, 1993).

4. Bridges, *Psalm 119*, 181–82.

5. Spurgeon, *The Treasury of David*, 304.

6. Ibid., 308; and Lockyer, *Psalms*, 569.

Chapter 7 The Eternal Word

1. Quoted by Joel R. Beeke and Ray B. Lanning, "The Transforming Power of Scripture" in *Sola Scriptura: The Protestant Position on the Bible*, ed. Don Kistler (Morgan, Pa.: Soli Deo Gloria Publications, 1995), 331–32.

2. Verse 90 is the second verse (following verse 84) that does not seem to mention the Scriptures specifically. But "faithfulness" probably refers to God's Word. The best argument for this is the parallel structure of verses 89–91, in which "your word," "your faithfulness," and "your laws" seem to be used as synonyms.

3. Spurgeon, *The Treasury of David*, 317.

4. Kidner, *Psalms 73–150*, 427.

Chapter 8 Loving God's Word

1. C. S. Lewis, *Reflections on the Psalms* (New York: Harcourt, Brace, and Company, 1958), 59–60. The whole discussion is on pages 54–65.

2. Kidner, *Psalms 73–150*, 427.

Chapter 9 The Clarity of God's Word

1. Exodus 40 is not the only chapter that mentions this unique phenomenon. It is also described in Exodus 13:21–22; Numbers 9:15–23; 10:34–36; and other passages.

2. Maclaren, *The Psalms*, 273.

Chapter 10 Walking by God's Word

1. Maclaren, *The Psalms*, 275.

2. Prothero, *The Psalms in Human Life*, 59.

3. David F. Wells, *No Place for Truth: Or Whatever Happened to Evangelical Theology?* (Grand Rapids: Eerdmans, 1993).

4. William Hazlitt, "On Persons One Would Wish to Have Seen" in *English Essays from Sir Philip Sidney to Macaulay* (Norwalk, Conn.: Easton Press, 1994), 295. In the original form of this essay, the speech is given to Leigh Hunt.

5. For example, in Psalm 38:17, 21–22; and Psalm 70:1–5.

Chapter 11 God's Wonderful Words

1. Neil Postman, *The Disappearance of Childhood* (1982; reprint, New York: Vintage Books, 1994).

2. Spurgeon, *The Treasury of David*, 378.

3. Ibid.

4. Martin Luther, *Luther's Works*, 500.

5. James Patterson and Peter Kim, *The Day America Told the Truth: What People Really Believe about Everything That Really Matters* (New York: Prentice Hall, 1991), 201.

Chapter 12 Using God's Word in Prayer

1. Notably in verses 23, 51, 61, 69–70, 78, 84–87, 95, 98, 110, 115, 121, 122, 134, and 139.

Notes

2. Kidner, *Psalms 73–150*, 428.

3. Spurgeon, *The Treasury of David*, 401.

4. Ronald A. Jenson, *Biblical Meditation: A Transforming Discipline* (Oakland, Calif.: ICBI Press, 1982), 11.

5. Ibid., 41.

6. H. A. Ironside, *In the Heavenlies: Practical Expository Addresses on the Epistle to the Ephesians* (Neptune, N.J.: Loizeaux Brothers, 1937), 86–87.

Chapter 13 Obedience while Waiting

1. Kidner, *Psalms 73–150*, 428.

2. John Charles Ryle, *Expository Thoughts on the Gospels: St. Luke*, vol. 1 (Cambridge: James Clark & Co., 1976), 195.

3. Spurgeon, *The Treasury of David*, 425–26.

4. "Peace" is linked to "salvation" even here, since verse 166 ("I wait for your salvation, O LORD") follows immediately on verse 165 ("Great peace have they who love your law, and nothing can make them stumble").

5. See Maclaren, "Submission and Peace" in *Expositions of Holy Scripture*, 329–35.

6. Saint Augustine, *The City of God*, in *A Select Library of the Nicene and Post-Nicene Fathers of the Christian Church*, ed. Philip Schaff, vol. 2 (Grand Rapids: Eerdmans, 1977), 500.

7. The monks used this verse as the basis for their observance of the seven hours for their prayer times. Chapter 16 of the Rule of St. Benedict reads, "This hallowed number of seven is fulfilled by us in this way: We perform the duties of our service at Matins, Prime, Terce, Sext, Nones, Vespers and Compline, because it was about these daily hours that he said, 'Seven times a day I have given praise to thee'" (footnote in Luther, *Luther's Works*, 525). Luther himself believed that the psalmist prophesied these canonical hours.

Chapter 14 This Poor Sheep

1. Kidner, *Psalms 73–150*, 429.

2. J. J. Stewart Perowne, *Commentary on the Psalms*, 367. Perowne concludes, "The figure, therefore, seems in this place to denote the helpless condition of the psalmist, without protectors, exposed to enemies, in the midst of whom he wanders, not knowing where to find rest and shelter." Leupold says the same thing. "He indicates nothing more than that his present situation is perilous like that of a sheep that has gotten beyond the shepherd's care" (H. C. Leupold, *Exposition of the Psalms*, 861).

3. Martin Luther, *Luther's Works*, 534.

4. C. A. Davis, cited in Spurgeon, *The Treasury of David*, 479.

5. See James Montgomery Boice, *Psalms: Psalms 1–41*, vol. 1 (Grand Rapids, Baker, 1994), 206–12.

6. Bridges, *Psalm 119*, 470.

7. Ibid., 480

8. Spurgeon, *The Treasury of David*, 440.